BOULDER CITY LIBRARY

3 1432 00196 852?

D0461055

J   Yomtov, Nel
954
.96   Nepal
YOM

Boulder City Library
701 Adams Boulevard
Boulder City, NV 89005

Nepal

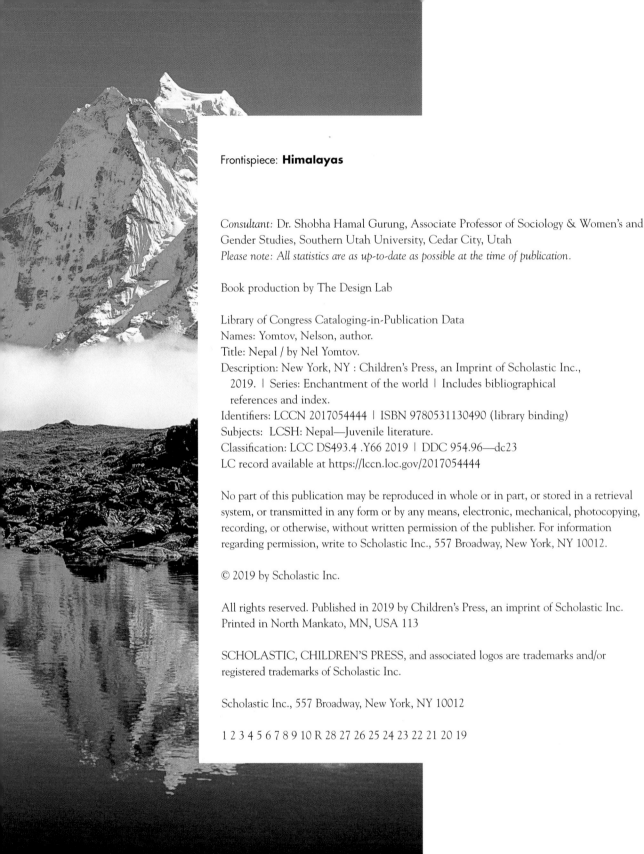

Frontispiece: **Himalayas**

Consultant: Dr. Shobha Hamal Gurung, Associate Professor of Sociology & Women's and Gender Studies, Southern Utah University, Cedar City, Utah
Please note: All statistics are as up-to-date as possible at the time of publication.

Book production by The Design Lab

Library of Congress Cataloging-in-Publication Data
Names: Yomtov, Nelson, author.
Title: Nepal / by Nel Yomtov.
Description: New York, NY : Children's Press, an Imprint of Scholastic Inc.,
   2019. | Series: Enchantment of the world | Includes bibliographical
   references and index.
Identifiers: LCCN 2017054444 | ISBN 9780531130490 (library binding)
Subjects: LCSH: Nepal—Juvenile literature.
Classification: LCC DS493.4 .Y66 2019 | DDC 954.96—dc23
LC record available at https://lccn.loc.gov/2017054444

No part of this publication may be reproduced in whole or in part, or stored in a retrieval system, or transmitted in any form or by any means, electronic, mechanical, photocopying, recording, or otherwise, without written permission of the publisher. For information regarding permission, write to Scholastic Inc., 557 Broadway, New York, NY 10012.

© 2019 by Scholastic Inc.

All rights reserved. Published in 2019 by Children's Press, an imprint of Scholastic Inc.
Printed in North Mankato, MN, USA 113

SCHOLASTIC, CHILDREN'S PRESS, and associated logos are trademarks and/or registered trademarks of Scholastic Inc.

Scholastic Inc., 557 Broadway, New York, NY 10012

1 2 3 4 5 6 7 8 9 10 R 28 27 26 25 24 23 22 21 20 19

Nepal

BY NEL YOMTOV

Enchantment of the World™
Second Series

Boulder City Library
701 Adams Boulevard
Boulder City, NV 89005

NOV 2018

DISCARD

CHILDREN'S PRESS®

An Imprint of Scholastic Inc.

Contents

Left to right: **Sal tree, Himalayan monal, rickshaw, prayer flags, festival mask**

CHAPTER I

Nepal Today

To some people, Nepal is a snowy land where mountain climbers battle the odds to reach the summits of the world's tallest peaks. Yet Nepal is far more than a playground for bold mountaineers. Squeezed between India and China, Nepal is one of the most diverse countries in the world. Its physical landscape ranges from forests to deep valleys to the spectacular peaks of the Himalayan mountain range. The variety of plant and animal life that exists in Nepal's distinct natural environments is spectacular.

Few countries on earth equal Nepal's cultural diversity. More than one hundred ethnic groups live within the relatively small territory, and about 120 different languages and dialects, or versions of languages, are spoken. Some Nepalese live in centuries-old cities lined with ancient Hindu temples and shrines. Others live in tiny mountain villages a stone's

Opposite: **Nepal is a young country. More than half the population is under the age of twenty-five.**

throw from Buddhist monasteries. The beliefs and practices of Hinduism, Buddhism, Christianity, Islam, shamanism, and nature worship peacefully exist side by side in Nepal, and they have for centuries. To most Nepalese and visitors, Nepal is a haven of spirituality.

Some of the appeal of this unique South Asian land is due to its relative isolation from the rest of the world. Nepal was never a colony, and its terrain and location kept it comfortably sealed off from the outside world.

And yet, as the twenty-first century unfolds, Nepal faces extreme challenges. It is one of the poorest nations in the world. There are few industries, and the county's farmland produces barely enough to feed the people. Nepal is forced to rely heavily on its neighbors, China and India, to meet its food, energy, and medical needs.

Nepal has been rocked by social unrest and political turmoil for many years. The country's long-standing monarchy was overthrown and the government has been frequently reorganized, resulting in political and economic chaos. As recently as 2006, an attempted takeover of the government by Maoists, followers of Communism, was barely avoided. A

A woman shakes out her scarf on a cliff edge near Pokhara, in central Nepal. Nepal has the second-highest average elevation of any country in the world, trailing only Bhutan, which also lies in the Himalayas.

Nepalese make their way through flooded streets in Lalitpur, south of Kathmandu, in 2017. The heavy rains in 2017 forced about 460,000 Nepalese from their homes.

new constitution adopted in 2015, the country's seventh in less than seventy years, has not yet delivered the peace it was intended to bring.

Nepal is also highly prone to natural disasters such as earthquakes, floods, and landslides. In 2015, an earthquake struck near the capital city of Kathmandu and the surrounding area. More than 30,000 people were killed or injured. Government buildings, ancient temples, homes, and businesses were destroyed. Tens of thousands of victims were left homeless, and without food, water, health care, and power.

In 2017, several days of heavy rainfall caused floods that

killed dozens of people. Nearly 50,000 homes were submerged under the rising waters. Experts estimated that nearly 80 percent of the nation's crops were destroyed. Nepal's extreme terrain and poor roadways in rural areas make rescue and relief missions a challenging task.

The new government of Nepal is working to introduce programs and projects that will rebuild the nation and put it on a path of economic growth and political stability. Despite the challenges, the people of Nepal welcome the future with hope and courage.

Ping-Pong is popular among teenagers in Nepal. Many tables are set up on the street.

CHAPTER 2

A Diverse Land

NEPAL, A SMALL, MOUNTAINOUS COUNTRY IN South Asia, is often described as a Himalayan kingdom. Lying mostly on the southern slopes of the Himalaya mountain range, Nepal is completely surrounded by land. China forms Nepal's northern border, while India lies to the west, south, and east.

Shaped like a long and thin rectangle, Nepal measures about 550 miles (885 kilometers) from west to east and 150 miles (241 km) from north to south. About 75 percent of the land is mountainous. Eight of the ten highest mountains in the world are found in Nepal, including the world's tallest peak, Mount Everest, which soars to 29,035 feet (8,850 meters) above sea level.

The geography of Nepal can be neatly divided into three main land regions, each spreading across the country from east

Opposite: **Brilliant blue lakes dot the Himalayas of Nepal.**

A man and his cows cross a broad river in the Terai.

to west: the low flatlands of the Terai; a band of moderate-sized mountains; and the towering Himalaya mountain range.

The Terai

The Terai region runs across Nepal's southern border with India. Dense, steamy jungles once covered the land, but few of these forests remain today. The Terai is a narrow strip of land about 20 miles (32 km) wide, yet the rich agricultural land found there provides Nepal with most of the country's food. Rice, corn, barley, potatoes, sugarcane, and tea are the major crops. Several rivers that originate in the Himalayas flow through the Terai. Nepal's lowest point, Kachana Kawal, which lies in the eastern Terai, is 230 feet (70 m) above sea level.

Though comprising a quarter of Nepal's land, the Terai is the country's most densely populated region, home to about half of all Nepalese. The Terai features several national parks and nature reserves, which are among the finest in Asia. Chitwan, Nepal's first national park, preserves forests and wetlands. Shuklaphanta National Park protects important grasslands and is a vital habitat for tigers, leopards, and other creatures. Unspoiled forests, grasslands, and rivers fill Bardia National Park.

Farther north in the Terai, marshes and forests begin to dominate the region as the land slopes upward toward more mountainous regions.

Chitwan National Park is one of Nepal's most popular tourist destinations. Many people who travel there go on elephant safaris.

Nepal's Geographic Features

Area: 56,827 square miles (147,181 sq km)

Highest Elevation: Mount Everest, 29,035 feet (8,850 m) above sea level

Lowest Elevation: Kachana Kawal, in the Terai, 230 feet (70 m) above sea level

Longest River: Karnali River, 315 miles (507 km)

Largest Lake: Rara Lake, 3 square miles (8 sq km)

Highest Average Temperature: Chitwan, with average July highs of about 92°F (33°C)

Lowest Average Temperature: Northern regions, with average January lows of 2°F (–17°C)

Highest Recorded Temperature: Chisapani, in the Kathmandu Valley, 114.8°F (46°C)

Lowest Recorded Temperature: Thakmarpha, in the Mustang District, –14.8°F (–26°C)

Rising Land

The Mahabharat and Siwalik mountain ranges are rocky, southern foothills of the Himalayas. Elevations in the hills are generally between 2,000 and 10,800 feet (600 and 3,300 m). Some peaks in the Mahabharat reach an imposing 12,000 feet (3,660 m). Swift streams and rivers run through steep gorges in the mountains.

Though agriculture here is less developed than in the Terai, farmers grow crops on terraces built on the slopes of the hills. Rice and corn are grown in the summer, with wheat and vegetables grown in winter. In the higher elevations in this region, potatoes and barley are the primary crops. Animals are raised for meat, wool, and milk.

This region includes several fertile, densely populated valleys. The Kathmandu Valley, located in central Nepal, is the historic and cultural center of the country. Home to

Houses sit among the terraced fields of rice in Nepal.

several of the largest cities in Nepal, including the capital of Kathmandu, the valley was a lake in prehistoric times. The waterways and mountains of the Pokhara Valley make it a popular destination for boaters, rafters, and trekkers.

The Himalayas

The rugged Himalayan mountain range stretches across northern Nepal. The Himalayas are not a single continuous range, but rather a series of large ranges. They are about 1,500 miles (2,400 km) long in total and pass through India, Pakistan, Afghanistan, China, Bhutan, and Nepal.

Mount Everest and nearby peaks pierce the clouds in Nepal.

Enchantment of the World **Nepal**

In Nepal, the Himalayas contain Mount Everest, the world's tallest peak, as well as seven other of the world's ten highest mountains: Kanchenjunga, Lhotse, Makalu, Cho Oyu, Dhaulagiri, Manaslu, and Annapurna. The people of Nepal regard the Himalayas as sacred, home of the most powerful Buddhist and Hindu deities, or gods. As a show of respect, mountain climbers often make offerings to the gods while trekking across the mountains.

Few people live in the cold, harsh climate of the mountain region. Inhabitants in the sparse settlements work as herders and traders. Farmers grow hardy crops such as barley and potatoes.

Rivers

About six thousand rivers and streams flow throughout Nepal. Most originate in the Tibetan Plateau north of the Himalayas and flow south into Nepal. They eventually flow into the mighty Ganges River in India and then into the Bay of Bengal, part of the Indian Ocean. River flooding is not a problem in the mountain regions, but serious floods frequently occur in the low-lying Terai flatlands. Nepal's three major river systems are the Karnali in the west; the Narayani in central Nepal; and the Kosi in the east.

Flowing 315 miles (507 km), the Karnali is Nepal's longest river. Rising in the southern slopes of the Himalayas in Tibet, the wild and rapid river runs through one of Nepal's most remote regions. After powering its way through deep mountain gorges, the Karnali reaches the Terai, where the river settles into a wide, gentle stream.

Deadly Quake

On April 25, 2015, a massive earthquake struck near the capital city of Kathmandu. More than nine thousand people were killed and many thousands more were injured during the quake and several powerful aftershocks. The earthquake was felt throughout Nepal. More than six hundred thousand buildings were destroyed, including important historical and cultural sites.

Nepalese search the rubble for their belongings following the 2015 earthquake.

The Narayani—whose name changes to Gandaki or Gandak farther south—slices through central Nepal. Older than the Himalayas themselves, the river is famous for its deep gorges cut into the mountains. Nepal's largest hydroelectric power plant, which produces electricity from the flowing water, is located on the river at the northern edge of the Mahabharat mountain range. Located nearby is Chitwan National Park, the nation's first national park, which was established in 1973. It is an important habitat for many creatures, including tigers, rhinoceroses, and sloth bears.

The Kosi River in eastern Nepal is known for its annual flooding during the summer rainy season. Waters rise as much as 30 feet (9 m) and make sections of Nepal and neighboring northern Bihar in India unsafe for living or agriculture. A dam at Barahakshetra was recently built to control flooding and provide hydropower to the region.

Nepal has an enormous potential for hydroelectric power.

The country's rivers and steep terrain provide ideal conditions for tapping Nepal's rich supply of water resources. The cost of building large hydropower plants, however, is high. As a result, Nepal has begun construction of many small hydroelectric plants.

Yaks are often used as pack animals high in the Himalayas of Nepal. They can withstand temperatures as cold as –40°F (–40°C).

Climate

Nepal's weather conditions are determined by two factors: elevation and the changes in precipitation caused by seasonal wind patterns, called monsoons. In the mountainous north, summers are cool, and winters are long and harsh with large amounts of snowfall. In the highest reaches of the Himalayas, snow remains on the ground year-round. In the southern plains of the Terai, summer temperatures often top 98 degrees Fahrenheit (37 degrees Celsius) and higher, while winter temperatures range from 45°F to 73°F (7°C to 23°C).

Nepalese light candles in memory of sixteen Nepalese guides who were killed in the 2014 avalanche on Mount Everest.

Danger in the Mountains

Climbing the high Himalayas is always dangerous, but the year 2014 proved to be particularly deadly. In April, sixteen climbers were killed in an avalanche on Mount Everest. The tragedy was the deadliest accident ever on the mountain.

Then, in October, severe blizzards and avalanches in the Annapurna region of east-central Nepal killed more than forty people. Most of the victims were trekkers and guides enjoying mountain climbs. More than five hundred people were rescued by airlift or by search-and-rescue teams on the ground. The tragedy made it clear that a system was needed to warn trekkers of poor weather conditions on the mountains.

Kathmandu Valley, which lies at an elevation of about 4,500 feet (1,370 m), has a pleasant climate with average summer temperatures of 66°F to 95°F (19°C to 35°C) and winter temperatures of 36°F to 54°F (2°C to 12°C).

During May and June, a dry, hot wind called the *loo* blows across northern India and the Terai region of Nepal. The loo reaches temperatures as high as 120°F (49°C) and can be deadly to humans, animals, and plants. The effect of the loo is most devastating in regions that have been stripped of forestland.

With no place to find shelter, birds and animals fall victim to high temperatures and arid air. The loo ends in the summer with the onset of the monsoon season. A monsoon is a shift in wind current that is accompanied by a change in rainfall. From October to early spring, the wind blowing into Nepal mainly comes from the north. From June to September, on the other hand, warm wet air blows in from the Bay of Bengal to the south. The warm air from over the water cools as it passes over land and falls as rain. Nepal receives more than 80 percent of its annual rainfall during the monsoon season.

Nepal's average annual rainfall is about 54 inches (137 centimeters), but it varies widely depending on the region. The Pokhara Valley, for example, receives about 132 inches (335 cm) of rain each year, while Mustang, a remote region on the northern border with China, receives less than 12 inches (30 cm) annually.

Young people dance in a rainstorm in Kathmandu. Most of the city's rain falls in the summer, with the humid monsoon winds.

Urban Landscapes

Kathmandu, the nation's capital, is home to about a million people. With a population of more than 400,000 people, Pokhara is Nepal's second-largest city. Pokhara lies at the foot of Annapurna on Phewa Lake. By the eighteenth century, it was an important stop on a trading route between India and China. Largely destroyed in a fire in 1949, the city was rebuilt and today is a popular tourist destination and a favorite spot for trekkers and adventurers. Also, Pokhara is home to large communities of Gurung and Magar peoples. Parts of the old city can be seen in the Purano Bazaar. The city features medieval temples standing side by side with modern yoga centers and restaurants. Pokhara also includes monkey-filled forests and snowcapped mountain peaks. Visitors can take a boat trip to the Tal Barahi, a temple shrine located on an island in Phewa Lake.

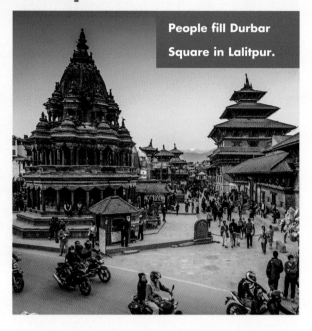

People fill Durbar Square in Lalitpur.

With its beautiful location, Pokhara is a popular tourist destination.

Located in the south-central part of the Kathmandu Valley is Lalitpur, Nepal's third-largest city, with a population of about 285,000. The city is also known as Patan. Lalitpur, which means City of Beauty, was likely founded around 300 CE by the Kirat dynasty. It is a major artistic center, featuring the woodcarvings and metalwork of the local Newar craftspeople. Ornate temples, courtyards, and shrines line the streets of the city center, Durbar Square. The square is also home to the Ancient Royal Palace, which was built during the 1600s. The splendid Patan Museum displays a vast collection of bronze and stone sculptures as well as woodcarvings that depict the impact of Buddhism and Hinduism on

Rows of brass bells hang at Dakshinkali Temple in Biratnagar.

Nepalese culture. The Royal Botanical Garden features handsomely manicured terraces with greenhouses and woods.

Bharatpur, the fourth-largest city, has a population of about 280,000 and is growing quickly. The city is a center for agriculture, particularly the production of chickens. Industry and tourism have grown in recent years. Many people travel to the city to visit nearby Chitwan National Park.

Home to 214,000 people, Biratnagar is the fifth-largest city in the country. Tucked up against the Indian border, it is the industrial center of eastern Nepal. The city has long been the center of Nepal's jute production industry. Jute is a vegetable fiber that is spun into coarse, strong threads used to make twine, rope, and matting. Today, steel production is a major industry in the city. Biratnagar's Dakshinkali Temple, dedicated to Kali, the Hindu goddess of creation and power, is a favorite pilgrimage destination. The nearby Koshi Tappu Wildlife Reserve is home to hundreds of animal species, including nearly five hundred species of birds.

Three-wheeled taxis called *tuk tuks* are a common form of transportation in Bharatpur and other Nepalese cities.

CHAPTER 3

Nature's Bounty

NEPAL'S DIVERSE CLIMATES AND ENVIRONMENTS are home to an amazing variety of plant and animal life. More than five thousand plant species are found in the country. Hundreds of species of mammals, reptiles, fish, amphibians, and birds inhabit the land and skies. From the tropical forests of the Terai to the chilly peaks of the Himalayas, Nepal is a wonderland of wildlife. Because of Nepal's dwindling forestland, however, many species are threatened or endangered there.

Plant Life

A few tree and plant species dominate the Terai. The robust sal tree grows in tropical forests below altitudes of around 3,000 feet (900 m). An important source of hardwood timber, its wood is used for buildings and furniture. Asna trees, which

Opposite: **The sal tree produces fruit that is used to make cooking oil and oil for lamps.**

A field of rhododendrons flowers near Mount Dhaulagiri.

The National Flower

The rhododendron is the national flower of Nepal. It grows as a flowering shrub and as a tall tree with large, bright flowers. About thirty varieties of rhododendron are found in Nepal. The most famous, *Rhododendron arboreum*, is known as Gurans in Nepal. At lower elevations, its flowers are a dazzling bright red. At higher elevations, pink rhododendrons grow. Even higher in the mountains, the flowers are a brilliant white. The delicate petals of the Gurans are used in foods, drinks, and traditional medicines.

grow to heights of 100 feet (30 m), can store water. During dry spells, villagers tap the trees to access the water. The bark of the asna is used as a medicine to treat stomach ailments. Other trees that grow in the Terai are different species of alders, evergreens, figs, and maples. Plants that flourish in the region include elephant grass and orchids.

In cooler, higher elevations, pines, oaks, bamboos, birches, firs, and chestnuts are common. Large tracts of rhododendron

Wood is a major source of cooking and heating fuel for many Nepalese.

trees grow in eastern and central Nepal at elevations ranging from about 4,500 to 12,000 feet (1,400 to 3,700 m).

In the northern mountain region, rhododendron, juniper, and other woody plants become prominent. Short grasses, mosses, and tiny plants grow in higher-altitude zones. No plant life exists beyond about 16,700 feet (5,100 m), the altitude where snow and ice remain year-round.

Disappearing Forests

Nepal was once covered in forestland. Today, about 40 percent of the land is forested. For centuries, people have cut down trees to clear farmland and obtain firewood and building materials. Animal herders have historically cleared tracts of forest to create space for their cattle to graze. Forests have also been cleared for the construction of roads, canals, dams, and power lines.

A mother and young rhinoceros stand in the grass in Chitwan National Park. Rhinoceroses, which are among the largest land mammals, are herbivores, meaning they eat only plants.

Nepal's disappearing forestland has damaged the country's ecology and economy. Deforestation results in soil erosion. Without plants and trees to hold the soil in place, it easily washes away. Eroded soil is carried to rivers where it fills the riverbeds, reducing the rivers' ability to hold water. This makes the land more prone to flooding. On steep mountain slopes, eroded soil slips and causes landslides. In addition, the removal of forests has destroyed plant and animal habitats. It has also decreased the amount of firewood available as a source of energy and building material. This has harmed the livelihoods of many Nepalese.

To protect its forests, the government has introduced a system that allows community groups to manage local land and use its resources most effectively. Each group develops its own forest management plan based on the needs of the community. Forest coverage in some areas using these groups has increased dramatically.

A Nepalese woman tends to one of her calves.

The National Animal

Nepal's national animal is the cow, an animal sacred to Hindus. In Nepal, cows are not raised for meat. In fact, the constitution makes it illegal to slaughter cows. Instead, they are used as work animals and raised for milk. Achham cattle, found in the Achham region of western Nepal, are the country's national breed. They are the smallest breed of cattle in the world, measuring less than 3 feet (1 m) high at the shoulder.

Diversity of Life

Nepal abounds with creatures of all kinds: mammals such as tigers, foxes, rhinoceroses, deer, and elephants; winged creatures such as pheasants, storks, and cranes; and countless river species such as carp, catfish, eels, and trout. Many species are endemic to Nepal, meaning they are found only in that country. Among them are the Chitwan burrowing frog, the Nepalese field mouse, the Rara snow trout, and the spiny babbler, a bird found mainly in the Kathmandu Valley. In total,

As mammals, Ganges River dolphins breathe air. They typically come up for a breath every 30 to 120 seconds.

A Rare Dolphin

Most dolphins live in salt water in the world's oceans, but there are four species of freshwater dolphins. These include Ganges River dolphins, which once thrived in Nepal's Kosi, Narayani, and Karnali river systems. The Ganges River dolphin has a long, thin snout. The creature is sometimes called a susu because it produces a "su-su" sound when breathing. Today, the calm, sociable mammal is on the brink of extinction. Pollution, overfishing, and the construction of dams have caused a steady decline in dolphin numbers. A 2014 survey estimated that only thirty Gangetic dolphins were still living in Nepal's rivers.

Nepal is home to more than two hundred species of mammals, nine hundred types of birds, one hundred fish species, and 170 kinds of reptiles and amphibians.

The Terai is Nepal's richest area for wildlife. In the south, buffalo, deer, tigers, leopards, monkeys, and wild oxen are found in the forests. Rhinoceroses, crocodiles, and Gangetic dolphins inhabit the rivers. Peacocks, ducks, and geese are found on the lakes, ponds, and rivers of the southern Terai.

The Himalayan wedge-billed babbler and the yellow-vented warbler are found in the sal forests. The Malayan night heron is a rare local species.

The lower mountains are home to small populations of black and brown bears, wildcats, wild boars, and muntjacs, which are also called barking deer. Farther north are serows and Himalayan gorals, two types of goatlike creatures. A variety of species of woodpeckers, thrushes, owls, and warblers inhabit Nepal's central region.

The number of Bengal tigers in Nepal has been increasing in recent years. Troops now patrol the national parks where the tigers live to prevent illegal hunting.

The cool, lower tract of the mountain region is home to snow leopards, musk deer, wild goats called tahrs, and marmots, a type of prairie dog about the size of a house cat.

Birdlife includes snow partridges, choughs, and buntings, small, colorful birds that resemble sparrows. Dippers and redstarts feed along the mountain streams. The high altitudes of the region are inhabited by danfes, also called Himalayan monals, the national bird of Nepal. These are a type of pheasant. Male danfes sport dazzling metallic colors of purple, copper, green, blue, and red. In the winter, large numbers of danfes can be spotted in the rhododendron forests.

Rhesus macaques are very adaptable. They can live in many environments, including cities.

A Visit to a National Park

The Sagarmatha National Park lies in the Himalayas of eastern Nepal. The area the park covers ranges in elevation from about 9,300 feet (2,830 m) in the southern reaches to 29,035 feet (8,850 m) at the peak of Mount Everest in the north. Established in 1976, Sagarmatha's natural beauty and spectacular mountain views make it a popular destination for tourists, trekkers, and wildlife lovers.

Majestic snowcapped peaks, glaciers, and lush, deep valleys dot the landscape of the park. Sagarmatha is also home to more than twenty villages of Sherpas, an ethnic group who lives in northeastern Nepal. Tengboche, a leading

The Himalayan monal has shiny, colorful feathers.

Trekkers in Sagarmatha National Park stop to admire Mount Everest.

Buddhist monastery of the Sherpa community, and other Buddhist monasteries host religious festivals throughout the year.

Hundreds of species of plants and animals live within Sagarmatha National Park. Pine, bamboo, and hemlock forests are found at Sagarmatha's lower elevations. Fir, birch, rhododendron, and juniper thrive at higher elevations. The park is home to several rare animal species such as the snow leopard and the red panda. Musk deer, langur monkeys, martens, Himalayan wolves, and pikas—a small, rabbitlike mammal—also live in the park. More than two hundred species of birds have been spotted in Sagarmatha, including Himalayan monals, snow cocks, blood pheasants, and the red-billed chough, a glossy black crow.

CHAPTER 4

Conquest and Independence

ALTHOUGH NEPAL HAS EXISTED AS A NATION FOR only about 250 years, its record of human habitation goes back far longer. Simple tools found in the Kathmandu Valley prove that humans existed in the region at least thirty thousand years ago.

According to legend, the Newar people have lived in Nepal the longest. Today, descendants of the Newars make up about half the population of the valley. In the centuries following the arrival of the Newars in what is now Nepal, many other peoples migrated there from other parts of Asia.

The Ancient Era

The Gopalas were the first people known to have settled in the Kathmandu Valley. They were nomadic cow herders who controlled the region roughly 3,500 years ago. The Abhiras,

Opposite: **This statue dates to the fifth century CE. It is located in the Changu Narayan temple near Bhaktapur. Changu Narayan is believed to be the oldest Hindu temple in Nepal in use today.**

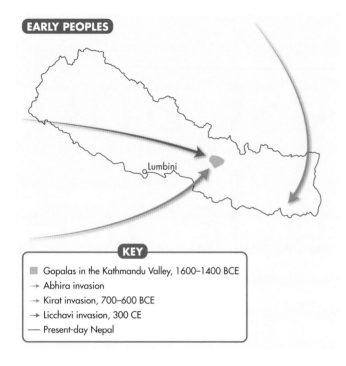

Lumbini

- Gopalas in the Kathmandu Valley, 1600–1400 BCE
- → Abhira invasion
- → Kirat invasion, 700–600 BCE
- → Licchavi invasion, 300 CE
- — Present-day Nepal

believed to have arrived from western and central India, conquered the Gopalas and ruled for around two hundred years. Sometime during the 700s BCE or the 600s BCE, a Mongolian group from the north called the Kirat invaded the eastern Terai and pushed westward into the Kathmandu Valley. The Kirat founded towns throughout central Nepal, where they extended their influence over other peoples in the valley. Commerce thrived under the Kirat as they traded metals, herbs, and woolen goods with people in other parts of Asia, including Tibet, India, and China. Siddhartha Gautama, the founder of Buddhism, was born in the Terai more than 2,500 years ago. He is believed to have traveled throughout the Kirat domain preaching his philosophy of proper living.

The long Kirat reign ended in about 300 CE when the Licchavis, Hindus from northern India, swept into the Kathmandu Valley. Under the Licchavis, the valley became an economic, cultural, and political center. Trade increased and arts and literature flourished. Religious tolerance became a cornerstone of Licchavi society as Buddhism and Hinduism flourished side by side.

In the eighth century CE, dominance in the valley shifted

Buddhist monks sit in the Sacred Garden, where Siddhartha Gautama is believed to have been born.

Birthplace of the Buddha

Lumbini, the birthplace of Siddhartha Gautama, known as the Buddha, is Nepal's holiest site. Located in the Terai, the 3-mile-long (5 km) complex of structures is the source of one of the world's great religions.

The Sacred Garden is believed to be the spot where the Buddha was born. At the time of his birth, it was a fruit grove. The centerpiece of the Sacred Garden is the Maya Devi Temple, which stands on the site of earlier temples. Maya Devi temple dates to 300 BCE, making it the oldest known structure in Nepal. The temple gets its name from Maya Devi, the Buddha's mother.

South of the temple is the Sacred Pool, where Maya Devi bathed before giving birth to the Buddha. Ruins of temples and monasteries around the pool date from the second century BCE to the tenth century CE. The Ashokan Pillar, the oldest monument in Nepal, lies west of the temple. The stone pillar was erected to record the visit of Indian emperor Ashoka in 249 BCE after he converted to Buddhism. Made of pink sandstone and standing 20 feet (6 m) tall, the pillar contains an inscription commemorating Ashoka's royal visit.

The Lumbini complex also contains ancient and modern temples and monasteries and a museum that houses clay sculptures, religious manuscripts, and coins. A bird sanctuary lies at the north end of the complex.

Durbar Square in Bhaktapur is filled with ancient temples and sculptures.

to the Thakuri people when the Licchavi king married his daughter to Amsuvarman, a Thakuri noble. Amsuvarman declared himself king when his father-in-law died. The new ruler established strong political and trade relations with China and Tibet. Learning, commerce, and the arts continued to thrive in Nepal.

The Malla Dynasty

In 1200, the Mallas rose to power in Nepal. Like the Licchavis, the Mallas were Hindus who tolerated Buddhism. The early centuries of Malla rule were marked by frequent military raids by Muslims from northern India. The Mallas fended off the invasions, and cities in the Kathmandu Valley, particularly Kathmandu, Patan (today's Lalitpur), and Bhaktapur, blossomed. As art, architecture, and learning thrived, the Malla era became a golden age in Nepalese history.

The prominent ruler Jayasthiti Malla established the kingdom's first legal code and introduced the caste system into Nepal. Under the caste system, a person's occupation and family status determined which of several social classes he or she was assigned to. The system is still in use in Nepal today, but the rules are not as rigid as they were in the past.

Yaksha Malla, who reigned from ca. 1429 to 1482, was the most influential of the Malla kings. He launched an extensive building program that included Hindu and Buddhist shrines and temples, as well as canals and irrigation projects. Yaksha also expanded the kingdom westward toward Gorkha; to the northwest; and eastward to present-day Biratnagar. Upon Yaksha's death, his kingdom was divided among his three sons, who were, according to Yaksha's wishes, to govern in cooperation with one another. For the next two centuries, however, Malla rulers—by this time cousins—became bitter rivals, and the once-great kingdom slowly crumbled.

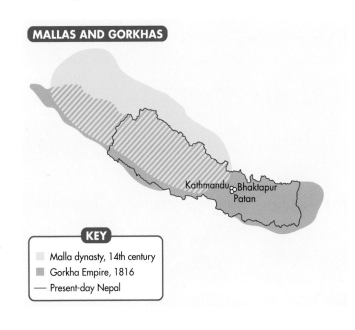

The Shahs of Gorkha

Prithvi Narayan Shah, the king of Gorkha, a small realm north of Kathmandu, observed the feuding Mallas and decided to invade the valley. The bloody war against the valley raged for twenty years. Finally, in 1769, Prithvi Narayan Shah conquered the valley's major cities—Kathmandu, Patan, and Bhaktapur. He established his capital at Kathmandu and unified the conquered territories into the modern state of Nepal.

In the following decades, Shah rulers expanded the kingdom through a series of military conquests. By 1790, Nepal had stretched its borders to northwestern and northeastern

In the 1500s, the Gorkhas built a palace that sits high on a cliff edge overlooking the Trisuli Valley.

India, nearly twice the size of the territory of modern-day Nepal. By the turn of the century, the powerful Nepalese army had helped make the country a leading power in Asia.

Conflict

Prithvi Narayan Shah's death in 1775 threw the young nation into a period of instability. Rivals in the royal court competed for control. Military power weakened, and the economy nearly collapsed. Despite the troubles, Nepal continued its campaign of territorial expansion—with alarming results.

Nepalese troops invaded Tibet, to the north, in 1788 and 1791. China, which controlled Tibet, sent a large army to oust the Nepalese. After defeating the invaders, Chinese forces

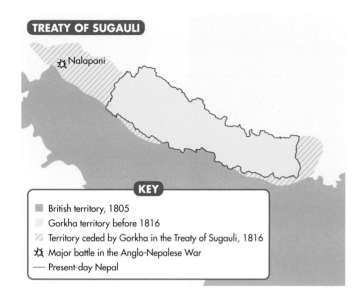

TREATY OF SUGAULI

☆ Nalapani

KEY

▦ British territory, 1805
▢ Gorkha territory before 1816
▨ Territory ceded by Gorkha in the Treaty of Sugauli, 1816
☆ Major battle in the Anglo-Nepalese War
— Present-day Nepal

entered Nepal. The Chinese forced the Shahs to return the conquered Tibetan territory and banned further Nepalese trade with Tibet.

Events were equally as threatening on Nepal's southern border. By the mid-1700s, traders of the British East India Company—Great Britain's official colonial agency—had established trading posts and forts in India. In 1814, fighting erupted between Nepal and Great Britain over a territorial dispute in the Terai. For two years, twelve thousand Nepalese troops held off British and Indian armies at the border. By early 1816, however, Nepal was forced to surrender. The Treaty of Sugauli ended the war. It not only gave Great Britain the right to install an official representative in Kathmandu but also shrank Nepal's territory to roughly its present size.

The Ranas

Nepal's military humiliations threw the Shah government into disorder and internal quarreling. In 1846, more than fifty members of the aristocracy vying for political power were assassinated near Kathmandu's Durbar Square. The mastermind behind the so-called Kot Massacre was an army commander named Jung Bahadur, who seized control and appointed himself prime minister for life. The king was stripped of his power. Bahadur and his descendants added "Rana" (roughly translated as "king") to their names and ruled Nepal for the next century.

Unlike other South Asian nations, Nepal remained independent under Rana rule. Relations with foreign nations, such as Great Britain and China, were strengthened. In 1923, Great Britain and Nepal signed a treaty that affirmed Nepal as an independent nation.

Troops rode elephants into battle during the war between Nepal and Great Britain.

The Ranas brought much-needed stability to the country. They did not focus, however, on public education and health. Most Nepalese could not read or write, and most lived in severe poverty. By the 1940s, opposition to the Rana dynasty was on the rise.

The Return of the Monarchy

In 1947, India gained its independence from Great Britain. Motivated by their neighbor's newfound freedom, Nepalese increased pressure on the Ranas to reform the government. The Ranas responded slowly. By late 1950, a full-blown rebellion, supported by the Nepalese military, emerged. In January 1951, the Rana prime minister reluctantly restored King Tribhuvan Shah, who had been living in India, to the throne of Nepal.

Jung Bahadur, the first Rana leader, and his wife. After becoming prime minister, Jung Bahadur had vast power within Nepal.

Tribhuvan's brief reign was ineffective. During some periods, the heads of various political parties held the post of prime minister and led the government. At other times, the

Edmund Hillary (left) and Tenzing Norgay (right) display the gear they wore when they conquered Mount Everest.

Top of the World

On May 29, 1953, Tenzing Norgay, a Nepalese Sherpa, and Edmund Hillary, an adventurer from New Zealand, became the first people to reach the summit of Mount Everest, the tallest peak on earth. The two climbers were part of a fifteen-man team that took part in the expedition. The successful ascent made international headlines. Both Norgay and Hillary were considered heroes.

Queen Elizabeth II of England knighted Hillary, but because Norgay was not a citizen of Great Britain, he received the lesser British Empire Medal. The government of Nepal gave their hometown hero 500 British pounds, a gift worth about $17,000 dollars today. In 1999, *TIME* magazine named Norgay and Hillary two of the most influential people of the twentieth century.

government was ruled directly by the king. Tribhuvan died in 1955. He was succeeded by his son Mahendra.

In 1959, King Mahendra Bir Bikram Shah Dev enacted Nepal's first constitution, which was based on those of Great

Mahendra was thirty-five years old when he became king.

Britain and India. The constitution established a two-house legislature, with a lower house elected by popular vote. Soon Nepal held the first democratic election in its history. The Nepali Congress Party (NCP) won the majority of the seats, and party leader B. P. Koirala became Nepal's first elected prime minister.

The new democratic government was short lived. Mahendra accused Koirala and the NCP of corruption and ineffectiveness. In December 1960, the king banned political parties, dissolved the Koirala government, and proclaimed himself the only ruler of Nepal. Koirala was arrested and jailed.

In 1962, Mahendra issued a new constitution that banned political parties. Instead, the government would be run by a system of nationwide village councils, or *panchayats*. Nepalese voters elected village councils, which in turn elected regional panchayats. The regional panchayats then elected members to serve on the National Panchayat. The king was granted near-absolute power and was free to change or suspend the constitution anytime.

The panchayat system resulted in progress and reform. Roads, bridges, irrigation systems, and power stations were built. The nation's education and public health systems were improved. The government also wiped out malaria, a deadly disease spread by mosquitoes, in the Terai. Though these

A young child is given a vaccine in a Nepalese village in 1963. The life expectancy of Nepalese has increased since the mid-twentieth century as health care has improved.

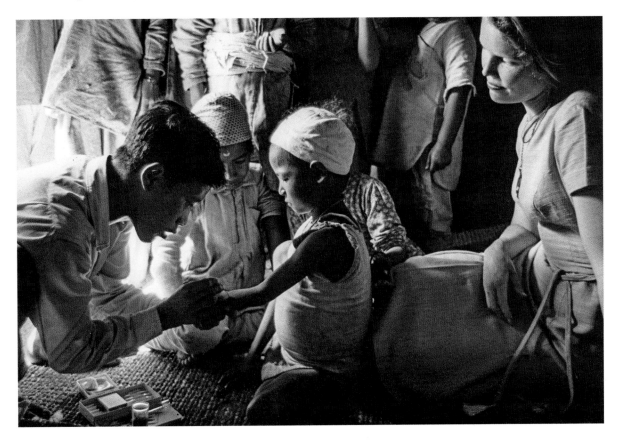

reforms resulted in agricultural and industrial growth, poverty and government corruption were widespread in Nepal.

The Struggle Continues

When King Mahendra died in 1972, his son Birendra Bir Bikram Shah assumed the throne. King Birendra supported the panchayat system, but he was opposed by many groups who were displeased with the lack of democracy in the nation. In 1979, riots by antigovernment demonstrators were brutally crushed by government forces. Birendra held a national vote

King Birendra and Queen Aishwarya greet Great Britain's Prince Charles on his visit to Nepal.

There were few cars in Nepal in the 1970s.

to decide whether to keep the panchayat system or return to the multiparty legislative form. Nepalese voted in favor of the panchayat system by a slim majority. Riots and mass demonstrations calling for fundamental freedoms continued throughout the country.

Birendra's political opponents pressed hard for reform. The NCP gained broader support, while various Communist parties were also growing. These parties wanted the government to take greater control of businesses and the economy. Several Communist groups joined to form the United Left

Front, which in turn merged with the NCP. In February 1990, several pro-reform groups launched the Movement for the Restoration of Democracy.

Birendra feared that the Shah monarchy would collapse. In response, he abolished the panchayat system and removed the ban on political parties. In April 1990, a temporary government was formed. It was made up of the two major opposition groups, the NCP and the United Left Front. The following month, national elections were held. The NCP won the majority of the seats, with many seats won by Communist

Communist Party of Nepal (Unified Marxist-Leninist) supporters celebrate electoral gains following an election in 1991. By this time, it was the second-largest party in Nepal's parliament.

and labor parties. A new constitution granting basic rights and a legislative democracy was soon adopted.

The new government failed to bring peace. In mid-1994, divisions within the NCP destabilized the country yet again. The legislature was dissolved and another election was held in November. Though no party held a majority, the Communist Party of Nepal (Unified Marxist-Leninist), or CPN-UML, won the most votes and formed a new government. Nepal became the world's first communist monarchy.

A Maoist rebel leader speaks to Nepalese villagers. The Maoists wanted to get rid of Nepal's monarchy.

Maoist Rebels

In 1996, Nepalese Maoists launched a revolt to overthrow the government and replace it with a communist government. Maoists follow the communist philosophy of China's Mao Zedong, which calls for revolution led by the working class. The Maoist rebels formed their own political party—the

The body of Queen Aishwarya is carried through Kathmandu. Hundreds of thousands of people filled the streets for the funeral procession.

Communist Party of Nepal (Maoist), or CPN-M—and used violence to promote their cause. Killings, bombings, kidnappings, and torture occurred throughout Nepal, particularly in rural regions. Attacks on government property, police, and civilians were widespread. Nepal was in a state of civil war.

As the violence raged on, the royal family suffered a shocking tragedy. In June 2001, King Birendra's son, Crown Prince Dipendra Bir Bikram Shah Dev, heir to the Nepalese throne, shot and killed his father, his mother, his brother, his sister, and five other relatives before killing himself. The shooting was sparked by a disagreement between the crown prince and his family over his choice of a bride. Following the slaughter, Birendra's brother, Gyanendra, became king.

The Chaos Continues

In 2002, the new king dissolved the legislature and took power for himself. He established several short-lived governments, but none brought harmony to the country. In 2005, Gyanendra declared a state of national emergency. He jailed many political opponents and ended freedom of the press.

A temporary constitution that gave executive power to the prime minister and limited the power of the king was adopted in 2006. The following year, the monarchy was abolished. In an election held in April 2008, the Unified Communist Party

Supporters of the Unified Communist Party of Nepal (Maoist) attend a protest in Kathmandu. It is one of the largest political parties in the nation.

of Nepal (Maoist), or UCPN-M, won the majority of the seats in the legislature. The new government voted to declare Nepal a democratic republic, ending nearly two hundred years of royal rule.

In the years since, governmental leaders have come and gone, and a new constitution was put into place. During this time of upheaval, the country had to deal with many natural disasters, including avalanches and floods. The worst, however, was the devastating earthquake of 2015. The quake left many neighborhoods, villages, and monuments in rubble. Much rebuilding remains to be done.

Laborers work to reconstruct a temple in Bhaktapur's main square, which was badly damaged in the 2015 earthquake.

Pushpa Basnet attends the CNN Heroes ceremony.

Modern-Day Hero

Pushpa Basnet is a lifesaver. She runs the Butterfly Home, a residence for children whose parents are in jail. Because of Nepal's weak economy, the government has few facilities for children in need. When poor parents in Nepal are arrested, they must choose between bringing their children to jail or allowing them to live on the streets with no supervision. In 2005, Basnet began running day care programs for children to receive education, food, and medical care. With the donations from friends, she set up a childcare center in a rented building. Every day, she picked up young children from prison and brought them to the center. She then returned the children to the prisons in the afternoon.

The Butterfly Home, located in Kathmandu, is a permanent home for older children. During school holidays, Basnet sends the children to visit their parents. She continues her hands-on care for the youngsters by bringing them food and fresh water during their stay. Basnet has helped more than 140 children of jailed parents. She has reunited about sixty children with their families upon a parent's release from prison.

Basnet has earned the admiration of many people and organizations around the world. In 2012, she won the CNN Hero of the Year award, given annually by the television network for outstanding work in humanitarian aid. Four years later, she won the CNN SuperHero award.

CHAPTER 5

The Democratic Way

NEPAL'S MOST RECENT CONSTITUTION WENT INTO effect in 2015. It established the nation as a democratic republic. This means that the citizens vote for people who represent them in the government. Nepal's constitution also established a federal system of government. Under this system, power is divided between the national government and regional governments. In Nepal, these regions are called provinces.

The Nepalese constitution outlines the basic rights of all Nepalese citizens, including religious freedom and the right to education, privacy, employment, housing, a clean environment, and health care, among others.

Like the United States government, the government of Nepal is composed of three branches: executive, legislative, and judicial.

Opposite: **Nepalese celebrate the adoption of the country's new constitution in 2015.**

K. P. Sharma Oli, the leader of the Communist Party of Nepal (Unified Marxist-Leninist), became prime minister of Nepal in 2018.

Executive Branch

The executive branch of Nepal's government includes the president, the vice president, the prime minister, and the Council of Ministers. The federal legislature and provincial assemblies elect the president for a term of five years. As head of state, the president's main task is to promote the country's national unity. Nepal's president serves mainly as a figurehead and does not oversee the day-to-day activities of the government.

The prime minister is the head of Nepal's government and the head of the executive branch. Appointed by the president, he or she is the leader of the political party with the majority

Nepal's President

Bidhya Devi Bhandari was elected the first woman president of the Federal Democratic Republic of Nepal in 2015. Born in eastern Nepal in 1961, Bhandari became politically active when she joined the Youth League of the Communist Party of Nepal (Unified Marxist-Leninist) in 1978. Prior to her election as president, Bhandari served as minister of defense and as minister of environment and population. She was also elected twice to the Nepalese parliament.

Bhandari is a strong supporter of women's rights and has pushed through a new regulation that ensures women make up at least one-third of Nepal's legislature. She has also focused on education, calling on the country's educational institutions to focus on teaching job skills. Among Bhandari's main tasks is to help rebuild the nation's roads, sewers, water supply system, and other facilities that were destroyed in the 2015 earthquake.

Bidhya Devi Bhandari was elected to a second term as president in 2018.

of seats in the House of Representatives. The prime minister appoints the members of the Council of Ministers. The council may contain no more than twenty-five members. Each minister in the council represents a different function of the federal government. These include finance, defense, labor and employment, energy, culture and tourism, youth and sports, and others.

Legislative Branch

Members of the Federal Parliament raise their hands to vote. One-third of the seats in Nepal's parliament are reserved for women.

Nepal's two-part legislative, or lawmaking, branch is called the Federal Parliament. It consists of the House of Representatives and the National Assembly. The House of Representatives is composed of 275 members. Of these, 165 are elected directly by the voters and 110 are elected through a system where voters vote for political parties. Members of the house serve five-year terms.

Nepal's Flag

Nepal's flag features two red right triangles with a blue border. A white crescent moon with rays coming out of it appears in the upper triangle, and a white twelve-pointed sun appears in the lower triangle. The color red represents the color of the rhododendron, Nepal's national flower, and the strength of the Nepalese people. The blue border signifies peace. The images of the sun and moon depict the hope that Nepal will last as long as those two heavenly bodies. The flag was officially adopted in 1962.

Nepal is the only country that does not have a rectangular national flag.

The National Assembly has fifty-nine members. An electoral college elects eight members from each of Nepal's seven administrative provinces. Three are appointed by the president on the recommendation of the Nepalese government. Members of the National Assembly serve six-year terms.

Judicial Branch

Nepal's judicial branch, or court system, is composed of the Supreme Court, the high court, and the district court. The Supreme Court, Nepal's highest court, consists of twenty judges and one chief justice. The president appoints the chief justice on the recommendation of the Constitutional Council, a body headed by the prime minister. The chief justice's term of office is six years. Other judges are appointed by the president

A woman casts her vote in a parliamentary election.

Nepal's National Government

Executive Branch

President

Vice President

Prime Minister

Council of Ministers

Legislative Branch

House of Representatives
(275 members)

National Assembly
(59 members)

Judicial

Supreme Court

Provincial High Courts

District/Local Courts

The National Anthem

"Sayaun Thunga Phool Ka" ("Made of Hundreds of Flowers") is the national anthem of Nepal. The lyrics were written by the poet Byakul Maila in 2006 to honor the newly declared Republic of Nepal and the end of the Shah monarchy. Amber Gurung composed the music for the new anthem.

Nepali lyrics

Sayau thuga phulka hami, eutai mala nepali.
Sarvabhaum bhai phailieka, Meci-Mahakali
Prakrtika koti-koti sampadako acala,
Virharuka ragatale, svatantra ra atala.
Jnanabhumi, shantibhumi Tarai, pahad, himala,
Akhanda yo pyaro hamro matrbhumi Nepala.
Bahul jati, bhasha, dharma, saskrti chan
  vishala,
Agragami rashtra hamro, jaya jaya Nepala!

English translation

Woven from hundreds of flowers, we are one
  garland that is Nepali.
Staying independent we have scattered from
  Mechi to Maharani
With the quilt of billons of natural heritages,
Independent and immovable because of the
  blood of the brave.
Land of knowledge, land of peace, Terai, hills,
  and mountains,
Indivisible, our loved motherland, Nepal.
Of many races, languages, religions, and
  cultures sprawl,
New is our country; hail, hail to Nepal!

on the recommendation of the Judicial Council, a body led by the chief justice.

There are seven high courts in Nepal, one in every province, the major regional divisions in the nation. High courts serve largely as courts of appeals, hearing cases tried in district courts in which a party is dissatisfied with the original verdict.

Nepalese protest an effort by parliament to impeach the chief justice of the Supreme Court. They argued that politicians were improperly interfering with the judiciary.

A Visit to the Capital

Kathmandu, Nepal's capital and largest city, is located in east-central Nepal in the Kathmandu Valley. Sitting about 4,600 feet (1,400 m) above sea level, Kathmandu has a temperate climate, with warm days and cool evenings and mornings. It is home to roughly a million people. The city was founded around 723 BCE. It became a major commercial and cultural center under the Malla kings. When the Shahs rose to power in the late 1700s, they made the city the capital of their new dynasty.

Kathmandu has been growing quickly in recent years.

Kathmandu is a diverse city featuring a blend of ancient Hindu and Buddhist religious sites, palaces, and sculptures standing alongside bustling restaurants and art galleries. The Old City is dominated by Durbar Square, which features Hanuman Dhoka, the Old Royal Palace, built in the seventeenth century. Also on the square is the nine-story Basantapur Tower, which was built by Prithvi Narayan Shah to honor the major cities of the Kathmandu Valley. Nearby is Kabindrapur Temple, also known as Dhansa. It is dedicated to the Hindu god Shiva and was built to stage dance and musical performances. The Tribhuvan Museum and the Mahendra Museum are popular sites where visitors can learn about the lives of Nepal's monarchs and glimpse royal thrones, furniture, and jewelry.

Kathmandu is a melting pot of ethnic groups. Newars make up roughly 30 percent of the population. Other significant groups include the Tamangs, Gurungs, Magars, and Chhetris. In recent years, many people from the Terai have migrated to Kathmandu.

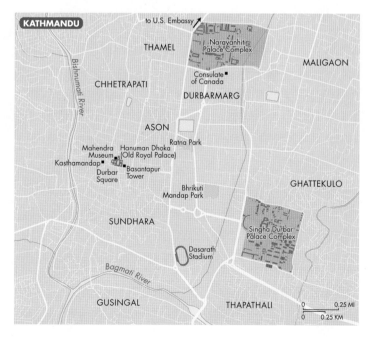

CHAPTER 6

Working Life

NEPAL IS ONE OF THE POOREST COUNTRIES IN THE world. The statistics tell the story. The average yearly income per person is only about $2,500, or roughly seven dollars a day. More than one-quarter of Nepal's people live on less than $14 per month.

Several factors have slowed economic development in Nepal. The rugged terrain makes transportation and construction difficult. Many isolated regions have poor services such as water, sewers, and other basic facilities. Political instability, civil war, and natural disasters have also made it difficult for the economy to thrive.

Agriculture

About 70 percent of all Nepalese work in agriculture, making it the largest segment of Nepal's economy. Agriculture

Opposite: **Workers pick tea leaves on a farm near Pokhara.**

Nepalese wait in line to get their documents to leave Nepal and work elsewhere.

Working Abroad

About three million Nepalese work in other countries. Usually they are employed in other places in Asia, most commonly Malaysia, Saudi Arabia, and Qatar. People who work abroad are central to Nepal's economy because they send money to their families. The money sent home is called remittances. In 2016, about 31 percent of Nepal's gross domestic product (GDP)—the value of all goods and services a country produces in a year—came from remittances. In no other country do remittances account for such a high percentage of the GDP.

accounts for roughly 30 percent of Nepal's gross domestic product, the total value of all goods and services produced in the country. Although agriculture is Nepal's most important economic sector, only about 28 percent of the land is suitable for farming. The majority of the farmable land is in the Terai. For the most part, Nepalese farmers work small plots of land and use traditional farming methods.

The crops grown in Nepal vary depending on region and climate. In the subtropical lowlands of the Terai, rice, wheat, barley, tobacco, and indigo are grown. In the temperate middle region, rice and corn are grown in the summer, and wheat, barley, and vegetables are grown in the winter. In the colder, higher northern mountains, potatoes, barley, and buckwheat are grown.

Other major crops grown in Nepal include lentils,

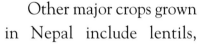

CHINA

NEPAL

Pokhara

Fe

Fe

Cu

Bharatpur

Kathmandu

Zn

Ls

Lalitpur

Cu

Ls

Cu

Ls

Cu

Biratnagar

KEY

Cropland	**Cu**	Copper	
Forest	**Fe**	Iron	
Grazing land	**Ls**	Limestone	
Rock and ice	**Zn**	Zinc	

INDIA

cabbage, beans, tomatoes, and coffee. Sugarcane, tobacco, and jute, a plant used to make rope, are grown on large farms. Yaks, goats, buffalo, and sheep are used as work animals or to provide meat, milk, and wool. More than half of Nepal's livestock is raised in the lower mountains between the Terai and the Himalayas.

Irrigation is rare in Nepal. Most of the irrigation systems are small or medium-sized. Farmers instead depend on the life-giving rains of the monsoon season to water their crops.

Industry

Until the mid-twentieth century, there was little industry in Nepal. Then, during the 1950s and 1960s, the government of Nepal operated businesses that manufactured products for sale to China and the Soviet Union. Most of these businesses used farm products such as jute and sugar as materials. In

Keeping It Simple

Tens of thousands of Nepalese make their livings as farmers on the steep hillside terraces of Nepal's lower mountains. Nearly all the work is done by hand. In recent years, many men who were once farmers have been migrating to cities to look for jobs. This often leaves the farming to girls and women who have less experience farming because they have traditionally done other tasks. In response, a Canadian research group called the International Development Research Centre and a Nepalese environmental organization called SAK Nepal have developed a simple yet effective form of help called Sustainable Agricultural Kits.

The kits contain inexpensive tools and seeds, as well as picture books that explain new planting techniques and basic farming practices such as weed control. The low-cost tools include garden gloves and handheld corn shellers to remove kernels from cobs. Use of the kits has increased productivity on farms and saved large amounts of labor per year.

A Nepalese woman uses a corn sheller.

the mid-1980s, the government began to promote industries that produced lumber, cement, paper, and bricks. Over the years, new policies were introduced to improve manufacturing efficiency. Despite the new measures, manufacturing has not grown significantly in Nepal. Today, industry, including

manufacturing and mining, employs roughly 12 percent of the nation's labor force.

There are many obstacles to expanding the industrial sector of the economy. The most important is the lack of electricity in many parts of the country. In addition, there are not enough skilled workers, and the low wages offered by manufacturers fail to attract people who are adequately skilled. Further, Nepal does not have enough raw materials to develop large-scale production.

Goods manufactured in the country include electronics, wooden furniture, leather products, soft drinks, beer, and soap. Nepalese factories also make metal, plastic, and rubber products. Carpets and pashmina shawls, which are woven from the hair of mountain goats, are made in large numbers.

Mining is a small part of Nepal's industry sector. Small-scale, privately owned companies mine marble, quartz, magnetite,

A worker shapes bricks at a factory near Kathmandu. The bricks are then laid out to dry and harden.

Oil Crisis

Nepal imports all its oil and many other essential goods from India. In 2015, Nepal accused India of blockading its deliveries to Nepal. India denied the claim, saying the disruption was due to political unrest in Nepal. Regardless of the cause, Nepal endured a severe oil and energy shortage. Because of the lack of gasoline, Nepalese schools were shut down. There were also shortages of medicines and of building materials required for reconstruction following the 2015 earthquake. By February 2016, the two countries had resolved their differences, but Nepalese still feared a future blockade.

salt, slate, talc, and limestone, the country's most important mineral resource. Gemstones unearthed in small quantities include garnets, rubies, and aquamarine. Among the metals mined in Nepal are nickel, lead, copper, and tin. Gold is mined in the Mahabharat range. The untapped resources of the upper Himalayas are believed to contain major deposits of silver, uranium, and gold.

Energy

With no developed oil, gas, or coal deposits, Nepal's energy sources are in short supply. Wood, animal waste, and other organic matter provide most of the energy Nepalese use for heating and cooking. Oil is imported from India.

Most of the nation's electricity is generated by hydropower. The country's rivers and steep terrain are ideal for producing hydroelectric energy. Dams are built on rivers, and then the swift-moving water is forced through turbines. The turbines spin, generating electricity. Since the early 2010s, the government has constructed many power plants and facilities to tap Nepal's vast hydropower potential.

The back of the 1,000-rupee banknote depicts an elephant.

Money Matters

The official currency of Nepal is the Nepalese rupee. The Nepalese rupee is divided into 100 paisa. Coins appear in values of 1, 5, 10, 25, and 50 paisa, and 1, 2, 5, and 10 rupees. The paper money, or banknotes, of Nepal comes in values of 5, 10, 20, 50, 100, and 1,000 rupees. The banknotes are brightly colored. On the front, they depict Mount Everest and famous Nepalese landmarks, and on the back they show animals that live in Nepal. For example, the 10-rupee banknote features Mount Everest and the ancient Hindu temple of Changu Narayan on one side and three bucks grazing on the opposite side. The banknote is colored brown, green, and lilac. The 50-rupee note, colored purple, green, and blue, depicts Mount Everest and the Janaki Temple in Janakpur on the front and a snow leopard on the back. In 2018, 104 Nepalese rupees equaled $1.00.

What Nepal Grows and Makes

Agriculture

Rice (2016)	5,226,647 metric tons
Corn (2017)	2,555,000 metric tons
Wheat (2016)	1,736,849 metric tons

Manufacturing (2016, value of exports)

Textiles	$235 million
Processed Foods	$122 million
Metals	$56.2 million

More tourists raft the Trisuli than any other Nepalese river. It offers exciting rapids and beautiful gorges.

Tourism

Tourism is central to Nepal's economy. The tourism industry employs more than 425,000 people and contributes more than $1.7 billion to the country's economy each year. The number of Nepalese working in tourism grows by the year.

Outdoor adventurers enjoy mountain climbing, trekking, bungee jumping, rafting, kayaking, hot-air ballooning, and much more. The nation's religious sites and monuments attract culture enthusiasts by the tens of thousands. In 2017, about 940,000 tourists visited Nepal. The largest number of tourists is from India, China, Sri Lanka, the United States, and Great Britain.

Volunteering tourism is a growing sector of the tourist industry. Following the 2015 earthquake and deadly floods

A Nepalese family orders lunch at a restaurant.

The Price in Nepal

	Nepalese rupees	U.S. dollars
Meal at an inexpensive restaurant	200	$1.95
1 gallon of milk	270	$2.60
1 dozen eggs	162	$1.57
1 head of lettuce	25	$0.24
Water (1.5 liter bottle)	35	$0.34
1 pair of brand-name jeans	3,400	$33.00
1 pair of men's shoes	4,200	$40.70
Movie ticket	350	$3.40

in 2017, volunteers from around the world traveled to Nepal to help rebuild the nation. Volunteers throughout the nation have served as teachers, doctors, and laborers, helping Nepalese recover from the disasters.

CHAPTER 7

An Ethnic Mix

NEPAL IS HOME TO MORE THAN 29 MILLION PEOPLE. Only about 19 percent of the population lives in cities, with the remaining 81 percent living in rural areas.

Roughly 95 percent of Nepal's total population lives in the hills region and the Terai. The Kathmandu Valley in the hills region is the most densely populated area in Nepal. It is growing at a rate of 4 percent each year, making it one of the fastest-growing urban centers in South Asia.

City and Village

Despite Nepal's large population, it has few big cities. Most Nepalese live in villages or smaller towns. The most populated region is the Kathmandu Valley and other parts of the hilly central region. In recent years, more people have been migrat-

Opposite: **A three-wheeled bicycle called a rickshaw carries passengers through a colorful street in Kathmandu.**

Population of Major Cities (2017 est.):

Kathmandu	
	975,453
Pokhara	414,141
Lalitpur	284,922
Bharatpur	280,502
Biratnagar	214,663

CHINA

NEPAL

Pokhara

Kathmandu

Bharatpur

Lalitpur

Biratnagar

INDIA

KEY	
Persons per square mile	Persons per square kilometer
more than 520	more than 200
260–520	100–200
130–260	50–100
65–130	25–50
26–65	10–25
3–26	1–10
fewer than 3	fewer than 1

Nepal's Ethnic Groups

Chhetri	17%
Brahman-Hill	12%
Magar	7%
Tharu	7%
Tamang	6%
Kami	5%
Newar	5%
Muslim	4%
Yadav	4%
Damai/Dholii	2%
Gurung	2%
Limbu	2%
Rai	2%
Thakuri	2%
Chamar/Harijan /Ram	1%
Koiri/Kushwaha	1%
Sarki	1%
Teli	1%
Other	19%

ing into the Terai. Few people live in the rocky, snow-covered mountains of the north.

Ethnic Groups

Nepal is home to more than one hundred different ethnic groups. The country's ethnic diversity came about after centuries of immigration mostly from Tibet and India to the north and the south. For the most part, Nepal's distinct geographic regions—tall mountains, steep valleys, and large tracts of forestland—have separated ethnic groups from one another.

People of the Terai

The Terai region is also called Madhesh, and the people who inhabit this flat southern area of Nepal are called the Madhesi. Roughly 70 percent of all people living in the Terai are Madhesis. The Madhesis include many ethnic groups, including the Rajbansi, Satar, Musalman, and Tharu, the largest ethnic group of the Terai region.

Tharus mainly live in the far western part of the Terai. Scattered throughout the jungle, they farm rice, corn, and lentils, and gather fruits and vegetables from the forest. Most Tharus are Hindu, but they incorporate traditional spiritual beliefs and medicine into their religious practices.

People of the Hills

The temperate climate of the middle region makes it home to Nepal's most diverse mix of ethnic groups. Among the people

Tharu people use large round nets to fish in shallow lakes and ponds.

Madhesi people attend a protest.

Independence for Madhesh?

For decades, Nepalese living in the Terai, or Madhesh, have claimed that the government has treated them as second-class citizens. Though they make up a large part of Nepal's population, Madhesis hold only 5 percent of government jobs, and they are not equally represented in the Nepalese parliament. Few Madhesis are given positions in the police and army. Until a recent change in the constitution, Madhesis did not even receive official citizenship cards.

Because of these problems, groups living in Madhesh have demanded their own independent state. Some pro-independence rallies and demonstrations have erupted into violence. Several groups, including the Terai People's Liberation Front, have committed criminal acts to bring attention to their demands. In August 2017, the Nepalese parliament rejected a bill to amend the constitution to improve treatment of Madhesh. The effort to achieve independence for Madhesh continues.

who live there are Newars, Gurungs, Magars, Kirats, Tamangs, Brahmins, and Chhetris.

The Newar people have lived in the Kathmandu Valley for more than two thousand years. Most Newars work as traders and shopkeepers. Some hold high political positions. Newars are predominantly Hindus, but some practice a form of Buddhism. Known for their skills as architects and craftspeople, the Newars were the builders of the famous temples, palaces, and monuments of Kathmandu.

The Gurungs migrated from western Tibet in the sixth century. They live in the central region around the Annapurna mountain range. Historically, Gurungs were animal herders and hunters. Today, military service and agriculture are their most important occupations. Some are successful businesspeople

A Newar farmer wears a hat called a topi. These hats are popular among many Nepalese ethnic groups, particularly in the hills.

CHINA

NEPAL

INDIA

KEY

Brahman-Hill	Magar	Sunwar
Chepang	Muslim	Tamang
Gurung	Newar	Tarai
Himali	Rai	Tharu
Limbu	Sherpa	Yadav

in the region's larger cities, such as Pokhara and Kathmandu. Gurungs practice both Hinduism and Buddhism.

The Magars dominate the hills of central and western Nepal. In the seventeenth and early eighteenth centuries, the Magar kingdom was one of the most powerful in Nepal. Like the Gurungs, many Magars were recruited into the British army in the years when Great Britain controlled South Asia, and many still serve in the Nepalese military. Farming, weaving, and fishing are the major occupations practiced by Magars. Traditionally, Magars are Buddhists, but many have adopted Hindu beliefs.

Descendants of the modern-day Kirats migrated from Tibet to the north and Myanmar to the east. Today, the Kirats live in the eastern hills extending across the border into parts of India. Most Kirats follow the religion of Kirat Mundum, a blend of the worship of nature and Tibetan Buddhism. The Kirats are known as great warriors. Many of them served in the British Gorkha regiments. Most Kirat communities are divided into tribes, which are subdivided into clans. Several different groups make up the Kirats. The largest are the Rai and Limbu people.

Members of the Tamang ethnic group live in the hills surrounding Kathmandu. In the Tibetan language, *tamang* means "horse trader." Tamangs are mostly Buddhists, but some also follow ancient religions. The Tamangs are the largest group of Buddhists in the country.

Brahmins and Chhetris are the largest of Nepal's ethnic groups. Though scattered throughout the country, they live mainly in the far west.

A Kirat woman wears traditional jewelry during a celebration of Nepal's many ethnic groups.

People of the Mountains

The people of the Himalaya region are descendants of arrivals from Tibet. They include the Sherpas and the Thakalis, among others. The Sherpas live in the Khumbu region of Nepal in the area of Mount Everest. Historically, Sherpas were traders and herders. Since the 1950s, they have gained international fame as mountain guides and baggage carriers. Sherpas follow the Buddhist religion.

Thakalis live in the Kaligandaki Valley in north-central Nepal. Many Thakalis are successful traders, and others own

Sherpas carry heavy loads high in the mountains. Most Sherpas live in the Himalayas, many at elevations of 12,000 to 14,000 feet (3,700 to 4,300 m).

hotels and restaurants along well-traveled trekking routes. Large numbers of Thakalis have recently resettled in Kathmandu and Pokhara to seek better job opportunities. Some work for the government. Younger Thakalis attend universities in the two major cities.

In the past, only people of a certain caste worked as police officers in Nepal. Today, these jobs are available to people of any caste.

Castes

In the past, Nepal had a traditional social structure known as the caste system. A caste system is a hierarchy based on religion and social rank. It established the types of occupation a person could have, his or her political power, and the social relationships he or she could have.

Brahmins were at the top of the Hindu caste system. Brahmins were the priests and scholars, and the only group permitted to read Hindu sacred writings. The Kshatriyas, or warrior class, worked in public service. Many served in Nepal's military or police forces. The Vaishyas were merchants and traders, and the Sudras were semiskilled or unskilled laborers. At the bottom of the caste system were the Dalits, or untouchables. They performed jobs considered "dirty," such as street sweeping. Traditionally, they could not enter temples or restaurants, or shop in certain public places.

Since democracy was introduced to Nepal, the caste system has become less common. Though it still exists in remote rural areas, it is nearly absent in the larger cities. It is now illegal to discriminate based upon caste. Lower classes have risen to take higher positions, such as important government jobs. And Brahmins and Kshatriyas have been

A line runs across the top of most Nepalese letters.

Common Nepali Phrases

Tapaaii lai kasto cha?	How are you?
Mero naam . . .	My name is . . .
Subha prabhat	Good morning
Subha ratri	Good night
Subha din	Have a nice day
Ho	Yes
Hoena	No
Maaph garnus	Excuse me
Dhanyabad	Thank you

engaged in traditional low-caste jobs such as washing clothes and selling meat and produce.

Language

More than 120 languages and dialects are spoken in Nepal. The official national language is Nepali. Nepali is an Indo-Aryan language similar to other languages used in the region, such as Hindi and Bengali, which are spoken in northern India. Many different dialects of Nepali are spoken throughout Nepal.

Nepali is written using the Devanagari alphabet, which has been in use since about 1000 CE. The Nepali language has eleven vowels and thirty-three consonants. Unlike English, each letter of the Nepali Devanagari alphabet represents only one sound.

After Nepali, the most widely spoken languages in Nepal are Maithili, Bhojpuri, Tharu, and Tamang.

CHAPTER 8

Ancient
Beliefs

A WALK THROUGH ANY CITY OR VILLAGE IN NEPAL will reveal that religion plays an important role in Nepalese life. Monasteries, temples, and shrines are found everywhere from the lowlands of the Terai to the highest, most remote peaks of the Himalayas.

Nepal grants religious freedom to all belief systems. Throughout the centuries, people who follow different religions have peacefully existed side by side in Nepal. The most recent constitution, however, makes it illegal to try to convert a person to a different religion.

Nepal's population is about 81 percent Hindu and 9 percent Buddhist. About 4 percent of the population is Muslim, followers of the religion Islam. A small portion of Nepal's population belongs to other faiths, including Christianity and groups that worship nature and their ancient ancestors.

Opposite: **A Hindu woman holds candles as part of a blessing.**

The Hindu deity Teleju is represented with four heads and ten arms.

Religion in Nepal (2009 est.)	
Hindu	81%
Buddhist	9%
Muslim	4%
Kirat Mundum (Shamanism)	3%
Christian	1%
Other	1%

Hinduism

Hinduism is considered the oldest religion in the world. With more than 1.1 billion followers, Hinduism is the world's third-largest religion, following Christianity and Islam. The roots of Hinduism date back four thousand years to the time when Aryan people migrated to India from central Asia. Over many centuries, the religious beliefs and practices of the Aryans and local groups blended to create Hinduism.

The holy books of Hinduism are called the Vedas. These are a collection of more than a thousand hymns, poems, and prayers. The Vedas were written in India sometime between 1500 BCE and 1000 BCE. Sanskrit is the language of the Vedas.

Hindus worship many different deities, but they are all manifestations, or forms, of the same god. The three principal

A small boy places a tika on a man in Kathmandu.

The Tika

The *tika* is a mark worn on the forehead as a sign of blessing from the gods. It may be worn after praying or on special religious or social occasions, such as marriage. The mark is created by applying a colored powder or paste to the forehead. Sometimes the substance is made from the sindoor tree, a sacred symbol of purity in Nepal. The tika is also called the "third eye." It symbolizes the doorway to inner wisdom and personal spiritual awareness.

deities are Brahma the Creator, Vishnu the Preserver, and Shiva the Destroyer.

Most Hindus believe in reincarnation, or the rebirth of the soul after death. They believe that when the body dies, the soul is reborn in another physical form, such as another human, an animal, or an insect. According to the concept of karma, leading a good life earns a person rebirth into a higher form. People are rewarded or punished in the future based on their good or bad actions of the past. Bad living sends a

A man creates a symbol called a mandala for a Hindu festival. The mandala represents the universe.

person back to a lower form. Dharma is the set of religious and moral rules that applies to one's station in life. If people follow dharma, they will gain merit and be reincarnated into a higher form in their next life. The ultimate goal of all Hindus is to continually be reborn into higher forms until one reaches *moksha*, a "oneness" with God.

Buddhism

Siddhartha Gautama, also known as the Buddha, founded Buddhism. He was born in Lumbini to rulers of the ancient city of Kapilavastu located in present-day southern Nepal.

As a prince, young Siddhartha lived a life of luxury and privilege. At about age twenty-nine, he began making trips to the countryside to learn what life was like outside the palace walls. Horrified to see the pain and suffering of the people, Siddhartha left home in search of solutions to what he had witnessed. After years of wandering, he came to understand the answer to the human condition and became spiritually enlightened. Now, as the Buddha—meaning "Enlightened One"—he began to preach his philosophies, called the Four Noble Truths:

1. The Truth of Suffering: Suffering comes in many forms, such as sickness and death. It also arises from the temporary satisfaction of desires. Pleasure does not last.

Symbols called Buddha Eyes or Wisdom Eyes are painted on most Buddhist temples in Nepal. Because they are painted on all four sides of a building, they indicate the all-seeing, enlightened nature of the Buddha.

2. The Origin of Suffering: The root of all suffering is desire, greed, ignorance, hatred, and violent urges.
3. The Ending of Suffering: People can eliminate the roots of suffering and free themselves from it.
4. The Path, also called the Middle Way: One can end suffering by following the Eightfold Path, which is right understanding, right intent, right speech, right action, right livelihood, right effort, right mindfulness, and meditation.

Buddhists light candles in preparation for a ceremony honoring a deceased religious leader.

A Nepalese sculpture of the Buddha

Words of the Enlightened One

The Buddha himself did not write any religious texts. His followers memorized his speeches and passed them down to later followers. The first written Buddhist texts, called sutras, appeared years after the Buddha's death. Many quotes have been attributed to the Buddha, including:

- Just as a candle cannot burn without fire, men cannot live without a spiritual life.
- To keep the body in good health is a duty . . . otherwise we shall not be able to keep our mind strong and clear.
- You will not be punished for your anger, you will be punished by your anger.

- What we think, we become.
- Peace comes from within. Do not seek it without.
- Hatred does not cease by hatred, but only by love; this is the eternal rule.
- Give, even if you only have a little.
- There is no fear for one whose mind is not filled by desires.
- Just as a snake sheds its skin, we must shed our past over and over again.

Prayer flags flutter in the wind in front of Annapurna.

Prayer Flags

Visitors to Nepal's Himalayan region are certain to notice large, colorful pieces of cloth fluttering in the mountain winds. These are known as prayer flags. Villagers string up the flags along mountain ridges and peaks so that the wind can spread their wishes for peace, wisdom, and strength.

Each colored flag represents an element found in nature. Blue represents the sky, white symbolizes the air and wind, red symbolizes fire, green is water, and yellow represents earth. Prayer flags are considered sacred objects, which must be carefully handled and treated respectfully. Some prayer flags contain holy writings and symbols that represent Buddhist beliefs and blessings.

Unlike Hinduism, Buddhism is not based on the worship of a god. Instead, it is a way of life that incorporates different beliefs, traditions, and practices based on the teachings of the Buddha. Buddhism accepts reincarnation. By following the teachings of the Buddha, a person will reach the enlightened state called nirvana—an end to the cycle of death and rebirth and an end to suffering.

Other Religions

Muslims have lived in Nepal for at least six hundred years. Most Nepalese Muslims live in the Terai. Many of them are poor and do not own land. Many other Nepalese Muslims live in Kathmandu. The five-hundred-year-old Nepalese Jame Masjid is the largest mosque in the Kathmandu Valley. It draws thousands of Muslims for weekly prayer.

Kirat Mundum is the religion of several Nepalese ethnic groups, including the Limbu and Rai, who live in the eastern hills. Kirat Mundum is an ancient belief system that involves the worship of ancestors, nature, and local gods. The spiritual leader in Kirat Mundum is called a shaman. The shaman is believed to be able to enter the spirit world, tell the future, and heal the sick. Some Nepalese mingle shamanism with their Hindu and Buddhist beliefs.

A Nepalese shaman performs a ritual in the mountains of central Nepal.

CHAPTER 9

A Rich Culture

NEPAL IS A MIX OF MANY DIFFERENT ETHNIC GROUPS, and its culture incorporates many different languages, religions, and traditions. The creativity and imagination of the Nepalese are proudly expressed in the arts, architecture, literature, music, sculpture, and dance of their nation.

Opposite: **Newars often wear masks for ceremonies, festivals, and dance performances. Many of the masks represent deities.**

Literature

Nepalese literature arose in the 1830s when the poet Bhanubhakta Acharya began translating the Hindu epic poem the *Ramayana* from Sanskrit into the Nepalese language. Sanskrit is the ancient language of Hinduism. Bhanubhakta, called the "first poet" of Nepal, also wrote poems about family and daily life in Nepal.

The early twentieth century ushered in the birth of modern Nepalese literature. Laxmi Prasad Devkota, considered one of

Nepal's greatest writers and poets, crafted memorable plays, short stories, novels, and songs. Many of his works deal with themes such as patriotism, injustice, and poverty in Nepal. His most famous work, *Muna Madan*, is a romantic epic poem that tells the story of a young man from Kathmandu who travels afar to seek his fortune. Published in 1935, *Muna Madan* is one of the best-selling books in Nepal.

Motiram Bhatta, who was born in 1866 in Kathmandu, was influenced by the work of Bhanubhakta and became a popular writer of essays, plays, and stories in the Nepali language. A

A Nepalese man is dressed like Hanuman, a deity who plays a major role in the *Ramayana*.

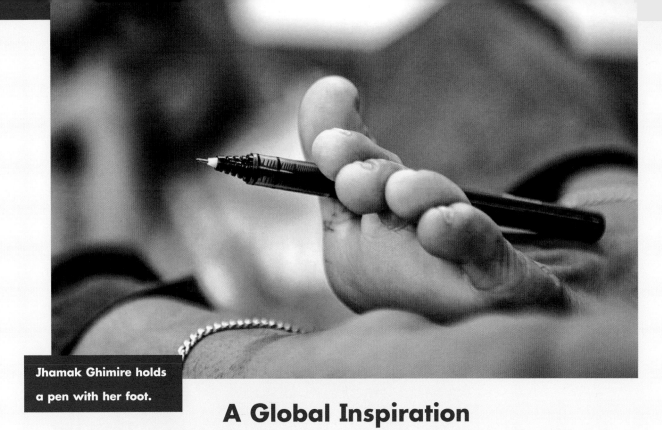

Jhamak Ghimire holds a pen with her foot.

A Global Inspiration

Jhamak Ghimire is one of Nepal's most celebrated modern poets and authors. Ghimire was born with a physical disability that robbed her of control of her arms and slurred her speech. Inspired by literature and poetry, she taught herself to write with her feet. Ghimire has written numerous books, including several collections of poetry. Her work explores political and social issues, and deals with emotions of love, regret, sorrow, and joy. Her collection of autobiographical essays, *A Flower in the Midst of Thorns*, won international acclaim.

musician and performer as well, Bhatta is credited as the person who established the first library in Nepal.

Contemporary Nepalese authors include Khagendra Sangraula, known for his satirical works. Buddhi Sagar's novel *Karnali Blues* earned international praise. Suman Pokhrel is one of the most prominent poets in South Asia. His works have been translated for a worldwide audience.

Many works of art in Nepal depict the Buddha.

Art

Traditional Nepalese art is devoted to religious themes. As early as the eleventh century, Newari artists illustrated religious manuscripts in a style based on Indian art. Newars also created *paubhas*, religious works that depict gods, monuments, and mandalas, traditional Hindu and Buddhist religious symbols. Using watercolor paints made from plants and minerals, skilled Newari artists created brilliant, colorful works. Their paintings featured rich reds, bright yellows, and deep, intense blue colors, often enhanced with glimmering gold and silver paint.

In the late thirteenth century, Newari artists visited Tibet and returned with a new art form called *thangka*, which depicts the Buddha and Buddhist themes. Most thangkas are painted on cotton or a delicate fabric woven from silk, and kept rolled up when not on display. The colorful art is highly detailed and elaborately designed.

A Nepalese artist paints a thangka.

Popular twentieth-century Nepalese artists include Chandra Man Maskey and Lain Singh Bangdel. Maskey, born in 1900, studied art in India. In 1940, after returning to Nepal, he was jailed for drawing an anti-Rana cartoon. He spent five years in jail. Upon his release, he taught art at a girls' high school and opened the short-lived Popular University of Kathmandu. He later served as a director of the Nepal National Museum.

Bangdel, born in 1919 in India, traveled to Paris and London to study art. He developed a nontraditional Nepalese style, and was asked by King Mahendra to launch a modern art movement

The city of Bhaktapur is renowned for its pottery.

in the country. Bangdel wrote a series of groundbreaking books on Nepalese art history, including *Stolen Images of Nepal*, which was published in 1989. The book accused high-ranking government officials of stealing valuable sculptures from the Kathmandu Valley between the 1960s and 1980s.

The National Museum displays art, artifacts, and weapons from throughout Nepal's history.

Architecture

Nepalese religious architecture is a significant part of the country's cultural heritage. Three styles dominate the architecture of Nepal: pagoda, stupa, and shikhara. The pagoda is a tiered tower often associated with China, but it actually originated in Nepal. In the late thirteenth century, a young Nepalese architect and sculptor named Araniko developed the pagoda style, which was later adopted in China. One

Boudhanath Stupa attracts Buddhist pilgrims from around the world.

of the world's most remarkable pagodas is Kasthamandap, a wooden structure in Kathmandu built during the Malla period. Pashupatinath Temple, northeast of the Kathmandu Valley, is another gem built in the pagoda style. Pagodas are most commonly Buddhist.

The stupa is a dome-like building used by Buddhists as a place of meditation or as a storehouse for religious relics. The Boudhanath Stupa in Kathmandu is one of the largest stupas in the world. It stands nearly twelve stories high and measures nearly 1,000 feet (305 m) across. Boudhanath is one of the most popular tourist attractions in Nepal.

The shikhara (Sanskrit for "mountain peak") style of Nepalese architecture features a tall, curved or pyramid-like tower topped with a bell shape. The Hindu Krishna temple in Patan's Durbar Square, built in 1637, is Nepal's finest example of this powerful, imposing style of architecture.

Music and Song

Traditional folk music is a vital part of Nepalese culture. Music traditions vary among the country's many ethnic groups, regions, and religions. More than one hundred types of musical instruments are played in Nepal.

Dohori music is a type of call-and-response folk song in which two teams of performers—boys in one group and girls in the other—"duel" one another with improvised lyrics and melodies. Verses are sung back and forth, first by the boys and then the girls, with flutes accompanying the dueling lyrics.

Folk music thrives in the hills region. The western

Buddhist monks play traditional instruments at a festival in Kathmandu.

A Nepalese boy plays a madal. The drum is typically made out of a hollowed-out log. The heads of the drum are made of goatskin.

hills resound with the sounds of *jhy-aure* music, which features the *madal*, a double-sided drum played horizontally with both hands. The Jyapu farming caste of the Newar people play lively rhythms on percussion instruments and woodwinds to accompany singing that has a nasal tone. *Selo* music comes from the Tamangs. It is played on a *damphu*, a large tambourine, and has been adopted by several non-Tamang communities.

Music is important to Hindu and Buddhist worship. *Bhajans* are Hindu songs that have religious themes, such as devotion to god or the teachings of a religious figure. Bhajans are sung individually or by large choruses. Some Buddhist rituals use nonmusical chants, while others feature a wide variety of wind and percussion instruments. In Buddhist monasteries in the remote regions of the Himalayas, monks play drums, horns, and cymbals, and blow through a conch shell during pauses in the prayer and chanting.

Sports

Soccer is the most popular sport in Nepal. Men and women play soccer in professional leagues, and both a men's team and a women's team represent Nepal in all international competitions. Dozens of teams compete at various skill levels in a variety of regional and national cup competitions. In 2016, Nepal's men's soccer team won the gold medal at the South

Young Buddhist monks play soccer in Pokhara.

Asian Games, defeating India in a thrilling final game.

Nepalese enjoy many traditional and regional sports. *Dandi biyo* is played in rural Nepal, using a 2-foot-long (0.6 m) stick and a 6-inch-long (15 cm) wooden pin. The game is played with two or more players. One player, the batter, uses the longer stick to launch the pin into the air, hitting it as far as possible. If the pin is caught by one of the fielders, the batter is out. *Kho kho* is a game of tag involving nine players on each team.

Kho kho teams from Nepal and Sri Lanka take part in a competition in India. The sport is popular throughout South Asia.

Mira Rai is Nepal's leading sports star.

Going the Distance

Mira Rai, Nepal's first female sports star, has experienced an extraordinary journey to the top of her profession. A national sports hero featured in children's books and depicted in murals throughout Nepal, Rai is a symbol of the Nepalese spirit of hardiness and adventure. Born to a poor family in the remote hills of eastern Nepal in 1988, Rai became a Maoist soldier at the age of fourteen during Nepal's civil war. When the war ended, she returned to her longtime passion: running. After months of training, she began her career in ultrarunning—a form of extreme distance running. Ultrarunnning events can cover 50 or 100 miles (80 or 160 km) and can last from forty-eight hours to six days. The athletes run across steep, rocky terrain. In 2014, Rai won her first trail race, a nine-hour dash through hail and blinding rain. That year, she won ten races and became an international running star. Rai has competed in trail races through Nepal's rugged Himalayan landscapes and in competitions in France, Spain, and Italy.

Other popular sports in Nepal are boxing, basketball, wrestling, volleyball, archery, and cricket, a bat-and-ball game that came to Nepal from Great Britain. Nepal has participated in the Summer Olympic Games since 1964 and in the Winter Olympic Games since 2002.

CHAPTER 10

Daily Life

NEPAL IS GEOGRAPHICALLY, ETHNICALLY, AND RELIgiously diverse. As a result, Nepalese culture includes a wide variety of foods and celebrations.

Food

The food eaten in Nepal has much in common with that eaten in nearby countries such as India and China. Ingredients such as root vegetables, tomatoes, lentils, potatoes, and lettuces are plentiful. Ginger, garlic, coriander, and cardamom are commonly used spices. Many hot dishes are cooked in mustard oil.

As in many other Asian countries, rice is a staple in Nepal. *Pulao* is a fried rice dish often made with vegetables seasoned with turmeric and cumin. It is typically accompanied with yogurt or thin, crisp treats made from lentils, rice, or chickpeas.

Opposite: **A grandmother and child work in a field in central Nepal. The average Nepalese lives seventy-one years.**

Dal bhat tarkari is considered the national dish of Nepal. This tasty meal of lentil soup, rice, and vegetables is often served with a curry made with chicken, fish, or goat meat. A spicy pickle called *achar* is sometimes included as a side dish. In some regions, a flatbread called *roti* replaces the rice and may be served with curry.

Dumplings called *momo* usually contain meat or vegetables. Other varieties of momo are made with cheese or potato. Momo are often served with a dip made with tomatoes. *Paneer* is a crumbly cheese eaten widely in Nepal. It is commonly made with milk and lemon juice or vinegar. *Chhurpi* cheese is made from buttermilk and is a favorite of Nepalese living in the Himalayan region.

Dal bhat tarkari often includes rice, bread, and several small dishes.

Clay pots filled with juju dhau for sale in Kathmandu

Juju Dhau: The King of Yogurt

In Nepal, yogurt serves more than one purpose. It is a delicious and nutritious food eaten every day, but it is also eaten to purify the body during religious ceremonies. *Juju dhau* is traditionally made with buffalo milk, which gives it a richer flavor than cow's milk. Have an adult help you with this recipe.

Ingredients
½ gallon whole milk
1/3 tablespoon cardamom
2 tablespoons plain yogurt
2½ ounces sugar

Directions
Pour the milk into a medium-sized frying pan and heat it on the stove to a simmer. Stir frequently. As the milk begins to thicken add the sugar and cardamom powder. Remove the frying pan from the heat and allow the mixture to cool. Add the yogurt and stir. Spoon the mixture into small bowls and cover each with tinfoil. Let the bowls sit overnight until the yogurt sets and hardens. Enjoy!

Momo is a common street food in Nepal.

Warm and comforting winter favorites include Gorkhali lamb and *thukpa*. Lamb meat is a rare treat in Nepal. Gorkhali lamb is a chunky curry dish made with lamb, potatoes, and roughly chopped onions. The lamb is often grilled and marinated in a chili mixture. Rice or roti make a tasty addition to the dish. Thukpa is a hot noodle soup, containing meat and vegetables. Goat or chicken meat is most commonly used to prepare the dish.

Education

Today, about two-thirds of Nepalese can read and write. This literacy rate may seem low, but it has been steadily on the

Shoes sit outside the door of a temple.

When in Nepal . . .

The Nepalese people follow certain social customs and rules of etiquette that may be unfamiliar to Americans. When in Nepal, follow these rules:

- Take off your shoes before entering a private home or a temple.
- Don't point with the finger, but instead use your entire hand or your chin.
- Use the right hand to eat, pass food, or receive and give gifts.
- Always walk clockwise around Buddhist religious sites.

- Public displays of affection between men and women are considered inappropriate.
- It is offensive to touch other people with your feet. When sitting in a group, avoid pointing the soles of your feet at another person.
- Hindus do not eat beef. It is permissible to eat beef in front of Hindu Nepalese, but do not offer it to them.

rise since the mid-twentieth century. In the early 1950s, only about 5 percent of Nepalese could read and write. In 1971, the Nepalese government introduced major education reforms. By 2011, the literacy rate had improved to 66 percent.

All schoolchildren in

Nepal wear uniforms.

In general, however, getting an education in Nepal can be difficult. This is largely due to the shortage of funds and qualified teachers. In rural areas, students must often walk great distances to reach a school.

Nepal's formal public education system consists of primary, middle, and secondary schools. Students attend primary school from age six to eleven. Middle education consists of three years, grades six to eight. Upon graduation, students may choose to attend a technical school rather than follow an academic path. Secondary education occurs in two phases. Grades nine and ten offer an academic schedule, while grades eleven and twelve offer opportunities to study subjects such as business, education, language, philosophy, and religion.

Higher education is offered at six universities. The government-funded Tribhuvan University (TU) is the nation's

A Nepalese couple gives each other tika marks as part of their marriage ceremony.

Marriage, Nepalese Style

Traditionally, most marriages in Nepal were arranged by parents, family members, and a *lami*, or matchmaker. When looking for a suitable partner, the lami will seek a person of the same caste or ethnic group. Marriages between castes are rare. Once the groom and bride are found, the parents will often visit an astrologer. The astrologer makes sure the couple's birth signs make for a good match. The groom and bride usually do not meet in person before their wedding day. Though the number of marriages in which young people choose their own partners is on the rise in Nepal, many marriages are still arranged.

oldest. With a population of several hundred thousand students, TU is one of the largest universities in the world. The institution offers classes at sixty campuses and more than one thousand smaller colleges across Nepal.

A girl dressed as a goddess rides in a chariot during the Indra Jatra festival.

Celebrations

Most festivals in Nepal are religious celebrations, usually honoring a god or goddess. Generally, Hindus and Buddhists celebrate separate holidays. Both groups, however, share some holidays. Among the most important festivals for Hindu Nepalese are Indra Jatra, Dashain, Tihar, and Teej.

Indra Jatra takes place in September, and is celebrated by both Hindus and Buddhists in the Kathmandu Valley. The festival is named after Lord Indra, the Hindu god of rain and the heavens. The eight-day festival begins with the raising of a colorfully decorated pole in front of the old Hanuman Dhoka Palace in Kathmandu. For several days, the chariot of Kumari, the Living Goddess, is carried through the streets. An ornately dressed girl, considered to be the reincarnation of the goddess Durga, rides in the chariot. The days are filled with joyous dancing, music, feasting, and prayer.

National Holidays

Democracy Day	February 18
Losar (Buddhist new year)	February
Maha Shivaratri (celebration of Hindu god Shiva)	February or March
International Women's Day	March 8
Festival of Colors	March
New Year's Day	April
Buddha Jayanti (Buddha's birthday)	April or May
Republic Day	May 29
Krishna's birthday	August or September
Teej	August or September
Indra Jatra (founding of Kathmandu)	September
Beginning of Dashain	September or October
Tihar (Festival of Lights) begins	October or November

On the Festival of Colors, also known as Holi, Hindus smear themselves and others with colored powders.

Dashain, celebrated in September or October, is the longest and most important national festival. The fifteen-day holiday celebrates the god Rama's victory over evil spirits. To prepare for Dashain, Nepalese clean and decorate their homes. People buy gifts and new clothing at local markets. Businesses and offices are closed, and people travel long distances to reunite with their families. On the ninth day of the festival each family sacrifices an animal—a goat, chicken, duck, or water buffalo—to honor the goddess Durga, who aided Rama's victory. In the streets, military bands play and guns are fired to commemorate the victory of good over evil. On the tenth day, Dashami, families gather to visit their elders and exchange gifts.

Garlands of marigold flowers for sale in Kathmandu. Nepalese decorate with marigolds during Tihar, the Festival of Lights.

Tihar, the Festival of Lights, follows Dashain. During this holiday, lamps are lit to honor Lakshmi, the goddess of wealth. During the five-day celebration, Nepalese pray for their brothers and sisters, and honor crows, dogs, and cattle. Children go from house to house in small groups and sing songs. In return, homeowners give the children money, fruits, and candies.

Teej is a festival that celebrates the women in Nepal. The festival honors the union of Lord Shiva and Goddess Parvati. On the first day of the celebration, married women gather with mothers, grandmothers, sisters, and daughters to enjoy a fine meal. On the second day, the women fast and offer prayers to Shiva and Parvati. The hours are marked by groups of women singing and dancing. They enjoy riding swings that are hung from trees and decorated with flowers. Married

Nepalese women dance during the Teej festival. Women typically wear red during the festival because in Nepal the color red represents good fortune and honor.

A traditional dancer performs in Kathmandu on Losar.

women decorate their hands with a dye called henna. The fast is broken on the third day.

The Buddhist new year festival, Losar, is celebrated for fifteen days. People wear their finest new clothes, exchange gifts, and socialize with family and friends. At Kathmandu's ancient Boudhanath Stupa, large crowds come together to sing, dance, and toss *tsampa*, or barley flour, as they ring in the new year. Prayer flags are strung around the enormous building. Monks pray and march around Boudhanath, performing religious rituals and ceremonies. Masked dancers act out battles between good and evil. Losar originated in Tibet in the seventh century BCE, long before the birth of Buddhism.

Buddha Jayanti, in April or May, celebrates the birth of Siddhartha Gautama, the Buddha, in Lumbini. Followers

Some bagh chal sets use pieces shaped like animals, while others use simple markers.

Move the Tigers!

Bagh chal, meaning "tigers moving," is a traditional board game played in Nepal and other parts of South Asia. It is a hunting game played by two people.

The moving pieces symbolize animals. One person plays four tiger pieces and the other plays twenty goats. The game board is a grid of boxes with lines the pieces may move along. The goal of the tigers is to capture the goats by jumping over them into an empty space. The goal of the goats is to surround the tigers so they cannot move or jump.

mark the day by discussing the life and teachings of the Buddha. At homes and monasteries, people decorate images of the Buddha with flowers. They also meditate and chant Buddhist holy texts. During this celebration, many people donate food, clothing, and money to the needy.

These and many other celebrations give Nepalese a chance to honor their traditions, express their spirituality, and enjoy special time with family and friends throughout the year.

Timeline

Nepalese History

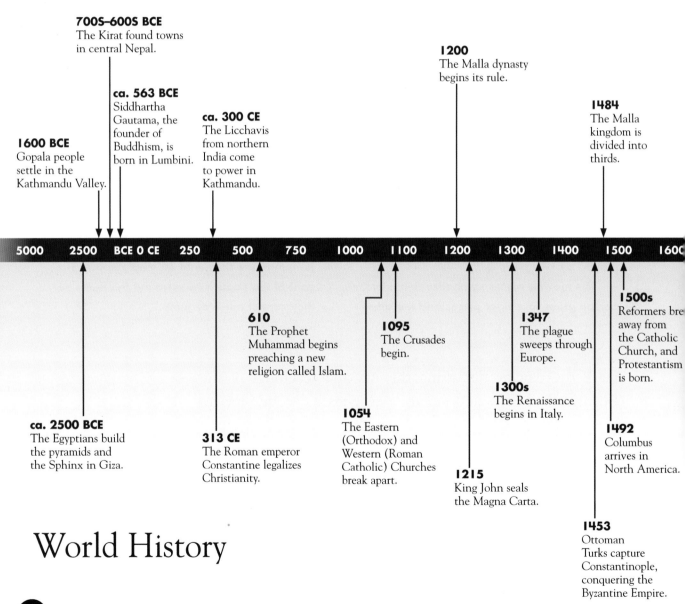

700S–600S BCE
The Kirat found towns in central Nepal.

ca. 563 BCE
Siddhartha Gautama, the founder of Buddhism, is born in Lumbini.

ca. 300 CE
The Licchavis from northern India come to power in Kathmandu.

1200
The Malla dynasty begins its rule.

1484
The Malla kingdom is divided into thirds.

1600 BCE
Gopala people settle in the Kathmandu Valley.

| 5000 | 2500 | BCE 0 CE | 250 | 500 | 750 | 1000 | 1100 | 1200 | 1300 | 1400 | 1500 | 1600 |

610
The Prophet Muhammad begins preaching a new religion called Islam.

1095
The Crusades begin.

1347
The plague sweeps through Europe.

1500s
Reformers break away from the Catholic Church, and Protestantism is born.

1300s
The Renaissance begins in Italy.

ca. 2500 BCE
The Egyptians build the pyramids and the Sphinx in Giza.

313 CE
The Roman emperor Constantine legalizes Christianity.

1054
The Eastern (Orthodox) and Western (Roman Catholic) Churches break apart.

1492
Columbus arrives in North America.

1215
King John seals the Magna Carta.

1453
Ottoman Turks capture Constantinople, conquering the Byzantine Empire.

World History

1846
Jung Bahadur Rana seizes control of Nepal's government; a century of Rana rule begins.

1959
Nepal adopts a multiparty constitution.

1990
The panchayat system is abandoned; a multiparty democratic government is established.

1960
King Mahendra seizes control and suspends parliament.

1996
A civil war erupts, with communist rebels fighting government forces.

2006
King Gyanendra reinstates the legislature, which votes to curb the king's political powers.

769
Gorkha ruler Prithvi Narayan Shah conquers Kathmandu and unifies the Kathmandu Valley.

1953
Nepal's Tenzing Norgay and New Zealand's Edmund Hillary become the first climbers to reach the summit of Mount Everest.

1951
King Tribhuvan Shah ousts the Rana prime minister and retakes the throne.

1962
A new constitution bans political parties and establishes a government system based on village councils, called panchayats.

2001
Crown Prince Dipendra kills several members of the royal family before killing himself.

2007
The monarchy is abolished.

1814–1816
Nepal and Great Britain fight the Anglo-Nepal War; the Treaty of Sugauli reduces Nepalese territory.

1923
Great Britain affirms Nepal as an independent nation.

2015
A powerful earthquake rocks Kathmandu, killing thousands; a new constitution is passed.

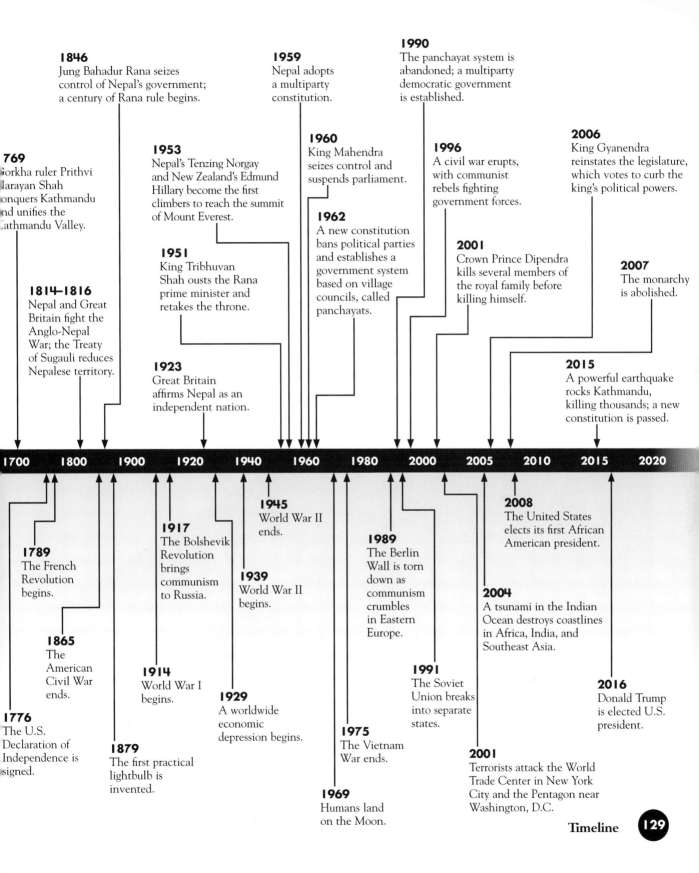

| 1700 | 1800 | 1900 | 1920 | 1940 | 1960 | 1980 | 2000 | 2005 | 2010 | 2015 | 2020 |

1945
World War II ends.

1917
The Bolshevik Revolution brings communism to Russia.

1989
The Berlin Wall is torn down as communism crumbles in Eastern Europe.

2008
The United States elects its first African American president.

1789
The French Revolution begins.

1939
World War II begins.

2004
A tsunami in the Indian Ocean destroys coastlines in Africa, India, and Southeast Asia.

1865
The American Civil War ends.

1914
World War I begins.

1929
A worldwide economic depression begins.

1991
The Soviet Union breaks into separate states.

1776
The U.S. Declaration of Independence is signed.

1879
The first practical lightbulb is invented.

1975
The Vietnam War ends.

2016
Donald Trump is elected U.S. president.

1969
Humans land on the Moon.

2001
Terrorists attack the World Trade Center in New York City and the Pentagon near Washington, D.C.

Timeline 129

Fast Facts

Official name:	Federal Democratic Republic of Nepal
Capital:	Kathmandu
Official language:	Nepali
Official religion:	None
National anthem:	*"Sayaun Thunga Phool Ka"* ("Made of Hundreds of Flowers")
Type of government:	Republic
Head of state:	President
Head of government:	Prime minister

Left to right: **Officers at attention, national flag**

Lake in the Himalayas

Area of country:	56,827 square miles (147,181 sq km)
Latitude and longitude of geographic center:	28°00' N, 84°00' E
Bordering countries:	China to the north; India to the east, south, and west
Highest elevation:	Mount Everest, 29,035 feet (8,850 m) above sea level
Lowest elevation:	Kachana Kawal, in the Terai, 230 feet (70 m) above sea level
Highest average temperature:	Chitwan, with average July highs of about 92°F (33°C)
Lowest average temperature:	Northern regions, with average January lows of 2°F (−17°C)
Average precipitation:	54 inches (137 cm) in Kathmandu

National population (2017 est.):	29,400,000	
Population of major cities (2017 est.):	Kathmandu	975,453
	Pokhara	414,141
	Lalitpur	284,922
	Bharatpur	280,502
	Biratnagar	214,663

Landmarks: ▶ *Boudhanath Stupa*, Kathmandu

▶ *Chitwan National Park*, Terai lowlands

▶ *Hindu Krishna Temple*, Lalitpur

▶ *Maya Devi Temple and Sacred Gardens*, Lumbini

▶ *Pashupatinath Temple*, Kathmandu

Economy: Agriculture is Nepal's leading industry and employs about 70 percent of the population. Fruits, vegetables, sugarcane, rice, wheat, and tobacco are the main crops. Other important industries include tourism, and carpet and garment manufacturing. India is Nepal's largest export partner, followed by the United States.

Currency: The Nepalese rupee (NPR) is the official currency of Nepal. In 2018, 104 Nepalese rupees equaled $1.00.

System of weights and measures: The metric system has been the standard system since 1968, though some units unique to the country are occasionally used.

Literacy rate: 66%

Common Nepali words and phrases:

Tapaaii lai kasto cha?	How are you?
Mero naam . . .	My name is . . .
Subha prabhat	Good morning
Subha ratri	Good night
Subha din	Have a nice day
Ho	Yes
Hoena	No
Maaph garnus	Excuse me
Dhanyabad	Thank you
Yo kati ho?	How much is this?

Prominent Nepalese:

Bhanubhakta Acharya	(1814–1868)
Poet	
Araniko	(1245–1306)
Architect and sculptor	
Siddhartha Gautama	(ca. 563–483 BCE)
The Buddha, the founder of Buddhism	
Tenzing Norgay	(1914–1986)
Sherpa mountaineer, climbed Mount Everest	
Mira Rai	(1989–)
Runner	
Gyanendra Shah	(1947–)
King of Nepal	

Clockwise from top: **Currency, Mira Rai, schoolchildren**

To Find Out More

Books

▶ Burbank, Jon, and Josie Elias. *Nepal*. New York: Cavendish Square, 2014.

▶ Helfand, Lewis. *Conquering Everest: The Lives of Edmund Hillary and Tenzing Norgay: A Graphic Novel*. New York: Penguin Random House, 2011.

▶ Mattern, Joanne. *Nepal*. New York: Cavendish Square, 2018.

Video

▶ *Buddhism*. Albany, GA: Smith Show Media Group, 2016.

▶ *High and Hallowed*. London: XTreme Video, 2015.

▶ *Hinduism*. Albany, GA: Smith Show Media Group, 2016.

▶ *Kathmandu Valley*. Tampa, FL: Travel Video Store, 2015.

▶ *Trekking in Nepal*. Tampa, FL: Travel Video Store, 2009.

▶ Visit this Scholastic website for more information on Nepal:
www.factsfornow.scholastic.com
Enter the keyword **Nepal**

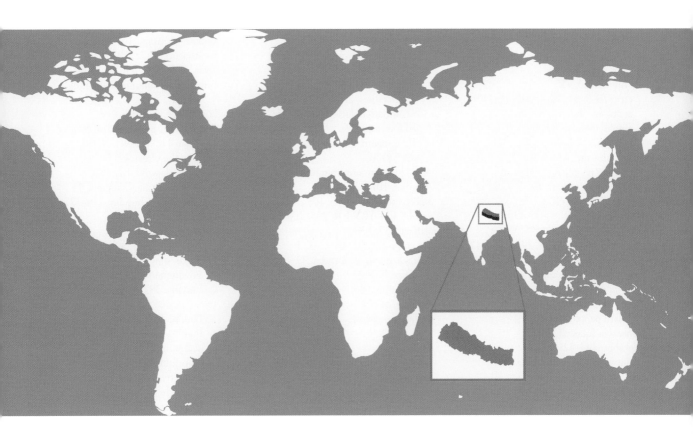

Index

Page numbers in *italics* indicate illustrations.

Meet the Author

NEL YOMTOV IS AN AWARD-WINNING AUTHOR WHO HAS written nonfiction books and graphic novels about American and world history, geography, science, mythology, sports, and careers. He has written numerous books in Scholastic's Enchantment of the World series, including *Scotland*, *Syria*, *Costa Rica*, *Israel*, *Russia*, and others.

Yomtov was born in New York City. He worked at Marvel Comics as a writer, editor, colorist, and director of product development. He has served as editorial director of a large children's book publisher and as publisher of the Hammond World Atlas book division. In addition, Yomtov was a consultant to Major League Baseball, where he helped develop an educational program for elementary and middle schools throughout the country.

Yomtov lives in the New York area with his wife, Nancy, a teacher. His son, Jess, is a sports journalist.

Photo Credits

Photographs ©: cover: Matteo Colombo/AWL Images; back cover: Christian Kober/Getty Images; 2: F1online digitale Bildagentur GmbH/Alamy Images; 4 left: Cheetah Zita/Shutterstock; 4 center: Jason Ondreicka/Dreamstime; 4 right: AlexBrylov/iStockphoto; 5 left: Frank Bienewald/LightRocket/Getty Images; 5 right: Beat Germann/Dreamstime; 6: hadynyah/ iStockphoto; 9: Christopher Villano/age fotostock; 10: PRAKASH MATHEMA/AFP/Getty Images; 11: Dimaberkut/ Dreamstime; 12: F1online digitale Bildagentur GmbH/Alamy Images; 14: Alex Treadway/Getty Images; 15: PRAKASH MATHEMA/AFP/Getty Images; 17: robas/iStockphoto; 18: Easyturn/iStockphoto; 20: think4photop/Shutterstock; 21: kaetana_istock/iStockphoto; 22: PRAKASH MATHEMA/AFP/Getty Images; 23: Tribhuz/iStockphoto; 24 bottom: Nabaraj Regmi/Dreamstime; 24 top: fotoVoyager/iStockphoto; 25 top: National Geographic Creative/Alamy Images; 25 bottom: Vladimir Zhoga/Shutterstock; 26: Cheetah Zita/Shutterstock; 28: Sushil Chettri/Dreamstime; 29: Patrice Correia/Dreamstime; 30: Jeff Foott/NPL/Minden Pictures; 31: Sergi Reboredo/VWPics/AP Images; 32: Roland Seitre/Minden Pictures; 33: Charles McDougal/ardea.com/age fotostock; 34: DOUGBERRY/iStockphoto; 35 left: Aurora Photos/Alamy Images; 35 right: Jason Ondreicka/Dreamstime; 36: Grant Dixon/Getty Images; 39: Frank Bienewald/imageBROKER/age fotostock; 40: laughingmango/iStockphoto; 42: LEROY Francis/hemis.fr/age fotostock; 43: Paul Fearn/Alamy Images; 45: The Print Collector/ Getty Images; 46: Maharaja of Nepal and his Wife, c.1870s (b/w photo), Bourne, S. (1834-1912) & Shepherd, C. (c.1858-85)/ Private Collection/Bridgeman Images; 47: AP Images; 48: James Burke/The LIFE Picture Collection/Getty Images; 49: Paul Conklin/The Granger Collection; 50: PA Images/Alamy Images; 51: Walter Rudolph/United Archives/UIG/Getty Images; 52: Robert Nickelsberg/The LIFE Images Collection/Getty Images; 53: Ujir Magar/AP Images; 54: DEVENDRA MAN SINGH/ AFP/Getty Images; 55: PRAKASH MATHEMA/AFP/Getty Images; 56: Joerg Boethling/Alamy Images; 57: Christopher Polk/ Getty Images; 58: Sanjog Manandhar/AP Images; 60: Narayan Maharjan/NurPhoto/Getty Images; 61: Narayan Maharjan/ NurPhoto/Getty Images; 62: Sunil Sharma/Xinhua/Alamy Images; 63: enigma_images/iStockphoto; 64: MANISH PAUDEL/ AFP/Getty Images; 65: Narayan Maharjan/Pacific Press/Alamy Images; 66: Narayan Maharjan/NurPhoto/Getty Images; 67: Mark Bennett/age fotostock; 68: Eitan Simanor/age fotostock; 70: PRAKASH MATHEMA/AFP/Getty Images; 72: SAKNepal Project/International Development Research Centre; 73: Dani Friedman/age fotostock; 75: Byelikova_Oksana/iStockphoto; 76: Alex Treadway/age fotostock; 77: Hemis/Alamy Images; 78: AlexBrylov/iStockphoto; 81: CORREIA Patrice/Alamy Images; 82: PRAKASH MATHEMA/AFP/Getty Images; 83: Om Prakash Yadav/age fotostock; 85: PRAKASH MATHEMA/AFP/ Getty Images; 86: Nicram Sabod/Shutterstock; 87: OlegD/Shutterstock; 88: Maggie Steber/Getty Images; 90: Julian Bound/ Dreamstime; 92: Feng Wei Photography/Getty Images; 93: Paul_Cooper/iStockphoto; 94: Dave Stamboulis/age fotostock; 95: Pisit Rapitpunt/Dreamstime; 96: Philippe Body/age fotostock; 97: Luciano Mortula - LGM/Shutterstock; 98: Frank Bienewald/ LightRocket/Getty Images; 99: CHARTON Franck/age fotostock; 100: Beat Germann/Dreamstime; 102: filmlandscape/ iStockphoto; 103: Jana Asenbrennerova/Nepali Times; 104: Nepal Images/Alamy Images; 105: Andrew Whitehead/Alamy Images; 106: Hemis/Alamy Images; 107: Wojtek Buss/age fotostock; 108: Anton_Ivanov/Shutterstock; 109: Niranjan Shrestha/ AP Images; 110: Jon Arnold/age fotostock; 111: Deddeda/age fotostock; 112: Shankar Mourya/Hindustan Times/Getty Images; 113: Mira Rai Collection; 114: Leonid Plotkin/Alamy Images; 116: Marquand, Michael/age fotostock; 117: Frank Bienewald/ imageBROKER/age fotostock; 118: Oliver Förstner/Dreamstime; 119: ©Studio One-One/Getty Images; 120: Tim Graham/ age fotostock; 121: sansubba/iStockphoto; 122: Narayan Maharjan/NurPhoto/Getty Images; 123: PRAKASH MATHEMA/ AFP/Getty Images; 124: Narayan Maharjan/NurPhoto/Sipa/AP Images; 125: Niranjan Shrestha/AP Images; 126: asiafoto/ iStockphoto; 127: Charles O. Cecil/Alamy Images; 130 right: enigma_images/iStockphoto; 130 left: Narayan Maharjan/Pacific Press/Alamy Images; 131: F1online digitale Bildagentur GmbH/Alamy Images; 133 top left: Byelikova_Oksana/iStockphoto; 133 bottom left: Tim Graham/age fotostock; 133 right: Mira Rai Collection.

Maps by Mapping Specialists.